BEHIND THE SCREEN

Uncover the Truth: Connect to your Power, Passion, Purpose!

Learn the 7-Step Life Timeline
System of Transformation

by
Carrie L. Schmidt

Copyright © 2022 by Carrie L. Schmidt.

All rights reserved. No part of this book may be reproduced or used in any manner without written permission of the copyright owner except for the use of quotations in a book review. For more information, contact: info@carrie-schmidt.com.

"Some quotes are from A Course in Miracles, copyright ©1992, 1999, 2007 by the Foundation for Inner Peace, 448 Ignacio Blvd., #306, Novato, CA 94949, www.acim.org and info@acim.org, used with permission."

Disclaimer

The author of this book does not provide medical advice or prescribe any method as a means of treatment for physical, emotional, or medical problems without first consulting a physician. The information offered in this book should not be treated as a substitute for professional medical advice. The intent of the author is to offer personal life lessons and information of a general nature to assist you on your journey of self-discovery and development. If you decide to use any of the information or suggestions provided in this book for yourself, the author and the publisher cannot be held liable or responsible for any loss, claim, or damage allegedly arising from your actions.

Portions of this book are works of nonfiction. Certain names and identifying characteristics have been changed.

ISBN Paperback: 979-8-9858613-0-3
ISBN Hardcover: 979-8-9858613-2-7
ISBN Electronic: 979-8-9858613-1-0
Library of Congress Control Number: 2022905464

Printed in the United States of America.

Infinite SOULutions Press
United States
www.carrie-schmidt.com

Dedication

I dedicate this book to my son, Caysen Ray Schmidt. I didn't realize the power behind your middle name until now. You are my "RAY" of light in this seemingly dark world. You were my awakening to love's presence. Your birth awakened my soul. You showed me what unconditional love really is. Your smile illuminates every room and brightens my day completely. Because of you, Caysen, I devote my life to helping others find their soul, their light, and the power of unconditional love. Thank you for being my Baby Bear. I love you with ALL my heart and soul. Remember, and always believe, "You can do anything you put your mind and heart to!"

Table of Contents

Acknowledgments	ix
Preface	xi
Introduction	1
A Future Outlook	5
Get to the Root of the Problem	6
Chapter 1: Welcome to the Program	9
Welcome!	10
A Journey of Transformation	15
Chapter 2: The Power of Your Mind	19
The Conscious and Subconscious Mind	20
Brainwave Frequencies	24
Mass Programming	28
Chapter 3: A System of Transformation	35
Awareness	36
The 7-Step Life Timeline System of Transformation	40
Step 1—TAG IT:	41
Step 2 – REMEMBER IT:	42
Step 3 – FEEL IT:	43
Step 4 – FLIP IT:	44
Step 5 – RELEASE IT:	44
Step 6 – REPROGRAM:	45
Step 7 – RESONATE:	45
Rinse and Repeat!	46
The 21/90 Rule	47
Chapter 4: The Download	49
Childhood Innocence	50
A Broken Family	53
Exercise: Step 1 – TAG IT!	58
Exercise: Step 2 – REMEMBER IT!	58
Exercise: Step 3 – FEEL IT!	59
Your Perspective	62

Chapter 5: The Teenage Screen — 65
- Searching for Love — 66
- A Broken Heart — 73
  - Exercise: Reflect upon Your Teenage Screen — 77

Chapter 6: Filling the Void — 79
- Unfulfilled Expectations — 80
  - Exercise: Projecting Unfulfilled Expectations? — 81
- The Escape — 82
- The Lonely Road — 85
- Misfit in Disguise — 86

Chapter 7: A Catalyst for Change — 89
- Egoic Illusions — 90
- Mental Health Crisis — 91
- Fitting into the Box — 97
- Fractal Patterns — 99
- An Invisible Force — 100
  - Exercise: The Looking Glass — 101

Chapter 8: Connect to your Power — 103
- The Great Discovery — 104
- Universal Consciousness — 108
  - Exercise: Infinite Possibilities — 118

Chapter 9: Paradox of Perception — 119
- Step 4 - FLIP IT — 120
  - Exercise: Step 4 – FLIP IT: — 124
- Change the Channel — 125

Chapter 10: Where There's a Will, There's a Way — 131
- The Beginning of the End — 132
- The Breath of Life — 134
- An Energetic Detox — 138

Chapter 11: Releasing Repressed Emotions — 147
- Step 5—Release It — 148
- Methods of Energy Release — 150
  - Exercise: Step 5 - RELEASE IT — 156

Chapter 12: Life Happens Between the Rise and Fall of it All — 157
- A Fresh Start — 158
- Everyday Evolution — 161
- The Struggle is Real — 166
- What Really Matters? — 167
  - Exercise: What Really Matters? — 169

TABLE OF CONTENTS

Chapter 13: Reprogram and Resonate	171
Creating a New Story	172
Step 6 – Reprogram	173
Exercise: Step 6 – Create a Vision	*180*
Step 7 – Resonate	181
Exercise: Step 7 – Become the New You	*185*
Chapter 14: Stepping into Your Truth	187
Accountability is Key	188
Positive Affirmations	190
The Wake-Up Call	191
Exercise: Take Action	*197*
Chapter 15: A Roadmap to Fulfilling Your Soul's Purpose	199
Ask, Act, and You Shall Receive	200
Love is the Way	204
Principles of the Program	208
The Voice of Truth	211
It's Your Time	212
Bibliography	225

Acknowledgments

To my Mom, thank you for always being there for me. I am sorry I allowed the resentment from my faulty program to steal precious moments during our journey together. Your love for Caysen and me has always been unconditional, just like mine is for him. You helped guide me along my life path to get into college, find my faith, and be the best mother I can be. Thank you!

To the Love of My Life, Tyson. Thank you for supporting and empowering me to continue my journey and make Behind the Screen a reality. You are my best friend, lover, and soulmate. I'm grateful for our spiritual growth, love, and miraculous connection. I look forward to spending the rest of our lifetimes together, traveling the world transforming lives, watching our children grow, and cherishing every moment as we all evolve spiritually.

To my BFF, Vicki. The Universe aligned our paths for a reason my friend! Thank you for always being there for me through thick and thin. I can't wait for you to introduce me on stages.

Preface

Dear Oprah,

My dream is to be interviewed by you! Just like you interviewed Mastin Kipp, Gabrielle Bernstein, Dr. Wayne Dyer, Marianne Williamson, and many other transformational leaders. I want to be a part of that list. I will be on that list.

I can, I will, I am.
This or something even greater still.

Sincerely,

Carrie L. Schmidt

I hold this vision and dream with an open heart, fueled by a burning desire and grateful expectation. Gram Madden, Aunt Joanne, and I used to watch *The Oprah Winfrey Show* every weekday after I got home from school, and when I appear on Oprah's show, I think Grandma Madden and Aunt Joanne will be proud.

Introduction

"Everything depends upon your perspective within your Life Timeline."
—Carrie L. Schmidt

It took an invisible virus to bring our world to a screeching halt. Our thoughts and feelings are invisible forces for greatness, but if we are unaware of this, we lose power. Humans have developed into unconscious beings—we are lost, distracted, disillusioned, and asleep at the wheel of life. We are stuck behind a screen—a program, a matrix of our perceptions and mirrored reflections. It's a holographic paradox within a veil of reality between our conscious and subconscious minds.

Your *Life Timeline* begins the moment you are born and runs into this present moment. How you view yourself, your life, others, and anything else is your "screen." Your way of thinking, point of view, beliefs, values, and ideals become your screen. Everyone has a screen. Memories, experiences, assumptions, perspectives. You can view it from many angles, and each perspective provides a unique experience. Over time, those experiences influence our decision-making, actions, and/or reactions to people/situations. Those actions or reactions may be conscious or unconscious, based on our level of awareness. Either way, they end up becoming our results.

Our *Life Timeline* becomes a series of unconscious thoughts, behaviors, and patterns that we inherited during the innocent "download phase" of childhood. Over time, we buy into the external things and events in our environment—commercials, trends, and the hype of the moment—whatever will fill our void. Instead of finding the reason for this void, we escape into food, alcohol, drugs, shopping, or other people to distract us from feeling the effects of it. Our pain, hopelessness, or loneliness hides behind a screen of shame, self-doubt, or denial. Our minds fuel the void, reinforced by the ego's perception that we need something from the outside to fill us up. Society has fooled us into believing the solution is outside of us.

In our relentless search for more, we become lost in illusions of perfection, separation, and instant gratification. Our world gives value and attention to the egoic mindset, and to a passion for riches and material things. Our search for more keeps the ego thriving, but ultimately leaves us feeling unfulfilled. We need more money to pay for closets full of clothes, name-brand shoes, violent video games, expensive cars, big houses, fancy watches, diamond rings. Our purpose becomes unclear. People feel they need to work hard (often in jobs they despise) to enjoy life's riches. But does material stuff really matter?

INTRODUCTION

We are like supercomputers walking through life on autopilot. We have lost our power. For generations, society and circumstances have slowly taken it away. We live in uncertain, trying times. The founding fathers of the United States of America built our country upon systems that are currently failing. Ideals, political corruption, social conditioning, conformity, and separation plague our world. Marriages don't last. We leave children to handle the broken pieces. Teenagers deal with acceptance issues, bullying, depression, anxiety, social media comparison, and other problems, all while trying to live up to someone else's expectations. Parents rush through each day with a To Do List that never ends while kids spend every moment possible consumed by electronics. Instead of consciously spending quality time with one another—we are distracted by things that are not fulfilling. We spend our time watching other people live their lives on social media. This new way of living, in a simulated reality, affects our mindset and ultimately our health and wellbeing in many ways. Distractions. Notifications. Too much to do with such little time. We live in a constant state of stress, plagued by fear and worry. We feel unfulfilled or defeated and endure each new day as if it will not be our last. Social unrest, injustice, unemployment, global warming, suicide, terrorism, a pandemic, travel bans, vaccination requirements… the list goes on and on. Between the rise and fall of it all, life happens. It is like someone—or something—is trying to deliver humanity a wake-up call.

I wrote this book to get you to see *Behind the Screen*, to reflect on your *Life Timeline* and identify unconscious behavior patterns that inhibit your ability to find peace, happiness, or the love you deserve. See the world, situations, and people from a different perspective. Remove your mask, open your mind and heart. As you read my personal stories and reflections *Behind the Screen* of my *Life Timeline*, discard judgment. It's easy to judge or criticize others—until you realize that behind the finger you are pointing at others, there are three fingers pointing back at you.

When we were growing up, we did not learn how to deal with issues that destroy families, and relationships. Prescriptions are more economical than therapy. Our minds and emotions run the show. They infuse energy into your environment. Your energy affects other people and vice versa. To answer life's wake-up call, we need to understand the power of our mind, body, energy, frequency, vibration, and our connection to all things in the Universe. Our children's and grandchildren's futures depend on our ability to raise our consciousness and "Connect to Our Power."

You were born with power. Babies are like angels on Earth; their innocence is intact. They have a will to live, breathe, and be loved. You and I do too, but as we grew up, we fell prey to someone else's agenda—we inherited faulty programs and conditions. Limitations were downloaded into our subconscious minds. Today, our subconscious operates our bodies ninety-five percent of the time. Hence, we are unconscious beings walking the planet, passing faulty programs on to our children. The cycle continues, generation after generation. Mental illness, racism, disease, broken homes, political power, wars, fights, and climate change are the effects. The cause? Our unconsciousness. But it's not too late. We can change. We can each influence the whole. Just as you have the will to live, you need the will to transform. When you transform your life, you affect other lives around you. It's a ripple effect—the power is almighty and universal—because **it's all energy**.

We are energetic or spiritual beings having a human experience. Many people are unaware of the invisible realm, but just as gravity is invisible and we know it exists, there are invisible forms of life out there and we know they exist. We can perceive things in our physical reality based on our five senses—but what about our sixth sense? What about the other ten dimensions, about which String Theory, a Quantum Physics model, gives us insight? Over the past century, science has uncovered so much information, it is mind-blowing.

When I was introduced to Quantum Physics, Neuroscience, and certain Universal Laws, I dove down that rabbit hole, researching and teaching myself what they hadn't taught me in school. Maybe it was their intention to keep us blinded from the truth that before anything manifests into our physical reality, it begins with an invisible thought or wave of probability. Our perspective can shift our reality!

What is real in our world? It's time we all dive into that rabbit hole and seek the knowledge we deserve to know about ourselves and the Universe. Let's shift our focus from the exterior, surface-level distractions to our interior, divine power. We need to get *behind the screen* and clean it.

A Future Outlook

As I write this book at thirty-eight years old, I imagine what my life will be like in twenty years. I will be fifty-eight; my thirteen-year-old son will be thirty-three! What a perspective to see! Time flies by in the blink of an eye. How old will you be in twenty years? How old will your kids be? Imagine it for a moment. Take a deep breath. Close your eyes. What does the world look like? Is there still a virus plaguing our lives? Do you need to show proof of vaccination to travel—or even work? What's the status of climate change and global warming? What happened to the school systems? How are people traveling? What is the form of currency? Is Taylor Swift performing as a hologram in multiple big cities at once? Are Google glasses and digital contact lenses the new screen? One thing is for sure, change is inevitable. The question we should ask ourselves is, "Are we doing our part to make sure the changes taking place in our lifetime are positive? The longevity of this planet is at risk. What are we doing to contribute to the solution for our children's sake?"

Get to the Root of the Problem

Some people think, "There is nothing I can do. The problems are too big for me to have an impact." Others say, "I can change my lifestyle and habits to influence the betterment of this world." Your perspective influences your reality and everyone else's since we share one home. I will introduce you to this transformational system, but only your will can clear you to proceed. You need to have the determination and desire to see the truth or get to the root cause of any problem. This is critical, because you cannot solve a problem until you understand the root cause of it. Once you understand the power of your mind and your subconscious programming from multiple perspectives, I will introduce you to the *7-Step Life Timeline System of Transformation*. I've spent years researching and practicing self-help systems and found these seven steps to be the most

INTRODUCTION

helpful in overcoming my own subconscious programming. This life-changing system will empower you—you will become mindful of your unconscious reactions to certain people and situations. You will start to notice the way you think and how it makes you feel. The system will help you bridge the gap between your conscious and subconscious minds, so you can become confident, passionate, and excited about the future. Gain the power to avoid getting triggered and overreacting in certain situations. The unconscious tendencies or behavior patterns affecting your current relationships or vocation took root a while back, likely during your childhood. You will notice that behavior and pinpoint its inception on your *Life Timeline*. As you progress through the seven steps in this book, you will overcome subconscious programming, release blocked energy, and reprogram a new state of being. You'll gain clarity, purpose, and passion to pursue your future goals and dreams. Are you ready to step into your greatness? To unlock your soul from the egoic screen and its control? Let's get started!

Chapter 1
Welcome to the Program

Welcome!

"Though we see the same world, we see it through different eyes." [1]
—Virginia Woolf

It's YOU.
Hi, meet ME.
ME, Meet, YOU.
It's a Mirror.
The SCREEN is your program.
It's your Lens of Life.
Your viewpoint of reality,
Personal reality or personality!
How you perceive me, and I perceive you.
True?
Our worldview,
The downloaded presumptions, beliefs, and memories,
Snapshots of sensations stored for later.
Experiences from a past that only you know.
The storage file for protection,
Or separation,
Which side of the screen are you watching?

WELCOME TO THE PROGRAM

What do you think somebody's life is like behind their pretty Facebook pictures or Instagram stories? Do you ever find yourself consumed with scrolling through social media news feeds or admiring or judging others? How do you perceive that picture-perfect family or their big, beautiful home? What do those gorgeous women look like behind the makeup, designer clothes, and Snapchat filters? If everyone took off their clothes and stood together naked, what would you see? The beauty or the ugly? Who decides that point of view?

Why do we compare ourselves to others and judge them based on the clothes they wear, their hairstyle, or their weight? Our perceptions and presumptions can be reflections of the internal compartmentalized insecurities that play out during our lifetime through the screen—like a metaphorical mirror. What is the mirror showing you? Your screen could be the doorway to greatness or the dungeon of your demise.

How you think others view you, versus their own screened view, is all a progressive creation in your mind. Whose view is right? Your mind is like a mirror reflecting a movie that is playing somewhere between your internal perceptions of yourself and the external environment. We can view our movie through a lens from multiple perspectives. Emotions fueled by experiences, signals, sounds, and other people's energetic forces drive our responses. Simplify every perspective down to the smallest common denominator and you get two sides: positive or negative. Love or fear. *A Course in Miracles* says that "Every choice you make is an expression of love or an expression of fear. There is no other choice."[2] We may know the expression of love as spirit, which gives off a positive vibrational frequency and allows your human body to view life through the lens of opportunity and infinite possibilities. We also know the expression of fear as the ego, which weighs you down by showing you all the things you should fear, doubt, or worry about. It leaves you stuck in a frequency of lack, negative energy, and low vibration. In this space, you cannot harmonize with anything greater. That's why you stay stuck, disconnected, longing for more. What is the source of this longing? What are we longing for? Love. Connection. Support. Friendship. Sense of purpose. I invite you to go deeper into these questions and reflect on the way they make you feel. Your feelings signify the energy you exude; they are your state of being. Most people don't realize that everything is energy—that it's all there is—an invisible realm of expanding and contracting energy. Balance and harmony are the goal. Our quest in life is for unconditional love, peace, joy, and happiness. We are all seeking the pot of gold at the end of the rainbow.

It's so simple, yet we overcomplicate, over-analyze, and defeat our own abilities, often unconsciously. Spirit empowers you to see your "Self" as beautiful and limitless, while ego leaves you feeling less than, always separate. The matrix is the program powered by the physical signals, invisible forces, and sources of information from a much larger faulty program. Maybe it's a simulation or a constant source of observation. What is real? What the news and social media tell us? What our parents taught us to believe? What we learned in school or based on our religion? What if that doesn't make sense? How do we find the truth? What is the truth? Your perception or mine? Who are "you"? Who am "I"? Dr. Seuss said it best, "Today you are You, that is truer than true. There is no one alive who is Youer than You."[3]

Let's explore these questions. I invite you to take a journey *behind the screen*, that veil of reality which exists beyond your five senses; the bridge between your conscious and subconscious minds. It can be the fight between your ego and spirit or the landscape between heaven and hell.

When you peel back the layers of that screen, you may observe pieces of the truth. Your way of thinking is a part of a *program*. You constructed it during your childhood while you learned your behavior patterns. We all develop our programs over time. They become part of who we are. They are your personal reality; a projection and reflection of the past in the present. Don't be afraid to uncover where you got your faulty program from. There are levels of conditioning that impact our daily lives and the decisions we make. The conditioning comes from society at large, from government and its institutions, and from laws and rules imposed upon us. People are trained to think, believe, want, and react in a way that is approved by the society in which they live. The training begins at birth. Behavior that is acceptable is rewarded, whereas typically, unacceptable behavior is punished. Over time, a person accepts this way of living and thereby becomes conditioned with their responses.

These macro-level social conditions mold people to behave according to someone else's expected way of living. For example, in the U.S., we are conditioned to choose a side—Republican or Democrat. Each side has their expectations for how the government should operate. Laws, regulations, and systems control how we live. Your parents, grandparents, family members, friends, and teachers pass micro-level social conditioning on to you. They teach you how you should think and act. These layers of conditioning form as we grow from children into teenagers and into early adulthood. Since the beginning of time, our way of life has been affected by that conditioning. Follow the leader and stay with the herd. This is known as herd-mentality. What if it were a ploy to make people unconscious? Unconscious of the power each of us holds? Racism, socialism, capitalism, alcoholism, Catholicism, terrorism—all the ism's. Ignorance. How well are you fitting into the box of cultural norms, religious rules, or family expectations? The impact could be positive, or it could be negative. Either way, the conditioning has been passed down to us for generations and it's taken root in the subconscious memory bank that drives our daily responses, often unconsciously. We will explore the power of the subconscious mind in Chapter 2.

It's up to you to notice your way of thinking, feeling, and acting now. Begin by reflecting on your *Life Timeline*. Notice the way your upbringing has affected your life—the rules imposed upon you, the values instilled in you, and the sense of self-worth you feel. Conduct an honest assessment of your relationships with others and yourself, your health and wellbeing, your academic or career accomplishments, and your overall sense of security and happiness. Ask yourself, "Where do I feel restricted or unhappy? In what area of my life do I long for something greater? Am I living my life to the fullest or am I being held back? What holds me back?" Answering these questions is the first step to connecting back to your power. Take over the wheel of your life. Steer in the direction you choose. It's your choice.

In every moment—in this moment—power exists, NOW. I encourage you to claim it. Assess your *Life Timeline*. What issues are you facing? Do you notice a feeling of resentment or disgust for someone in your life today? Do you attract the same type of person and ultimately, the same types of results in your romantic relationships? I attract the bad guys. I get hurt. What can you learn from this experiential feedback? If you look deeper, under all the layers of life, what would you find? A lost little girl yearning for love? Does something from your past hold you back from achieving greatness? I am sure there is something coming up for you. We all have memories, experiences, and emotions that have become a part of building our character and who we are. That's life. However, if they are inhibiting your ability to live a peaceful, joyful, and healthy lifestyle, it's time to release their bonds on your being. You can overcome your subconscious tendencies and change the trajectory of your life now. Whether or not you realize it, your unconscious behavior patterns have affected your relationships. Your parenting style could reflect how you were brought up. Every day, your mindset affects your health and wellbeing. The growth or decline of your career depends on your ability to control your reactions. The way in which you interact with other people and the choices you make can reflect the way you were raised. Our life is a reflection on repeat, based on our emotional experiences—until, that is, you become conscious of your state of being in each present moment and Connect to your Power.

I didn't always know this. For years I walked through life, unconscious of the power that was breathing me, depressed, praying for other people to change. I was questioning my purpose and reason for being alive, trying to figure out why I seemed to always run into trouble. It was like I had a black cloud following me around. Was I cursed or just putting myself in the wrong circumstances? Was it me or them? Should I follow my heart or my head? Hang out with this crowd or that one? Should I care what other people say about me? The battle between right and wrong can rip a hole of worry right through your stomach while the butterflies escape into the chaotic storm your analytical mind has stirred up.

A Journey of Transformation

I am so happy and grateful to lead you on this transformational journey. It's NOT easy for me to share my truth. In fact, it's terrifying. Even so, I will not hide behind my screen. By sharing my stories, the memories, pain, and realizations, I hope to have an impact on your life. If I can provide you with the confidence to walk in your truth, see past your perceived limitations, and rise above judgment, criticism, or insecurities, every word I write is worth it.

My program has been stuck on the channel of judgment and ridicule for decades. To lead a better life, I have had to change the channel and tune into my intuition. I took the time required to journal my thoughts, feelings, and experiences in order to see certain trends that played out over my life. I started looking for information to help make sense of the obsessive thoughts and constant worry that plagued my mind. I tagged my program and decided that it was time to make a change. I took action by signing up for a self-development program offered by Mary Morrissey and the Life Mastery Institute. The Dream Builder Program provides twelve weeks of content that help you transform your dreams into reality. This program changed my life and my way of thinking about everything. It helped me overcome my own conditioning and focus on the truth that we are spiritual beings having a human experience. It led me to Los Angeles to study with Mary Morrissey and other Life Coaches from around the world. I found the power of self-love, faith, and forgiveness, which enhanced my ability to overcome my screen of shame and share my truth.

Nobody is perfect. We place ourselves in an ocean of comparison. Don't get stuck at the bottom of the ocean, allowing waves to crash your dreams and destroy your passion to pursue a better life. Fear will not hold me back from sharing realizations and strategies that may help you. It's all just a program, anyway. Throughout this book, you'll learn that we aren't so different after all. In fact, everything and everyone is connected.

WELCOME TO THE PROGRAM

I will share my experience as a child dealing with my parents' divorce, and later, the effects of racism, family abandonment, depression, anxiety, and self-sabotaging behavior that drove me through the mud of trouble right into my moment of awakening. Through my stories, I'll share strategies I used to overcome my screened view of the world, override the subconscious program, and connect to my power. You'll identify where your past is holding you back from having the abundant future you dream of. Isolate the blocks held within your energy body or subconscious and release them. You'll shift your way of being and put a stop to self-sabotaging patterns. Are you ready to begin this life-changing system of transformation? It is time to flip the screen and look in the mirror to see what's on the other side.

Everything is a matrix of your perception. "Mirror, mirror, on the wall, who is the highest above us all?" It's consciousness! The higher power, the great I AM—the soul—is seeking a greater expression of itself through your physical body. It's the essence of life that gives you passion and ignites your aura with glowing, positive vibrations. This energy that you feel is life-giving, soul-feeding, immune to any virus, and connected to the Source of Creation. It's your power. Source energy. Spirit. You are a spiritual being—perceiving this world through the five senses of your human body. There's so much we don't know about our internal capabilities, the power of our mind, our connection to all things in the universe through energy, frequency, vibration, and spirit. It's ever expanding and alive, pulsing like our heart beats. Humans sense the connection, but the ego holds us back from realizing the truth. We identify ourselves by what we have, which forces us to want more. My mentor, Dr. Wayne Dyer, refers to the EGO as "Edge God Out." I remember this acronym anytime I think about the concept of the ego.

In this book, we identify how ego has edged God out of our lives. I let down my guard, open my heart, and share with you the feelings and experiences from my past replayed by my subconscious mind. The programmed way of thinking and reacting within situations of my life will be a baseline for you to compare your way of living or state of being to. *Behind the Screen* is at once a journal, a work of art, and a window into my soul. A reflection of memories, thoughts, feelings, and realizations throughout the evolution of my life poured out onto these pages over many days, nights, dreams, and transformational moments. It's taken over three years to write this book, and I have realized a lot about myself during the process. While those realizations are priceless, if my story can have a positive impact on at least one person's life, my soul has served its purpose on this earth. I believe that the content revealed in the following chapters will benefit high school and college students profoundly as well as their parents. A revolutionary system of transformation for the entire family—what could be better?

Welcome to the Program, my friend. I invite you inside the capsule of secrets, priceless information, and wisdom from *Behind the Screen*, which will feed you infinitely. As a bonus, I've included a complimentary *Life Timeline Journal* (which you can find at the back of this book) to record all your notes and personal discoveries. Please familiarize yourself with the *Life Timeline Journal* now. As you read through chapters in the book, there are exercises that ask questions for you to reflect on over your *Life Timeline*. Allow yourself time to reflect after reading each chapter. You can use the journal to capture your own thoughts, feelings, memories, and realizations as you progress through each of the seven steps. If you are hungry for more out of life, you have made the right choice to read **Behind the Screen!**

Chapter 2
The Power of Your Mind

The Conscious and Subconscious Mind

> "An excellent way to get acquainted with the two functions of your mind is to look upon your mind as a garden.
> You are a gardener, and you are planting seeds (thoughts) in your subconscious mind all day long, based on your habitual thinking.
> As you sow in your subconscious mind, so shall you reap in your body and environment." [4]
> —Joseph Murphy

Let's explore the power of the mind. According to The Editors of *Encyclopedia Britannica*:

> ...mind, in the Western tradition, the complex of faculties involved in perceiving, remembering, considering, evaluating, and deciding. Mind is in some sense reflected in such occurrences as sensations, perceptions, emotions, memory, desires, various types of reasoning, motives, choices, traits of personality, and the unconscious.[5]

These mental faculties direct your responses throughout your *Life Timeline* and play a critical role in everything you do, reflecting your results. The mind has two main parts—the conscious and the subconscious. Your conscious mind is about five percent active, while your subconscious makes up ninety-five percent of your brain's capacity. When you pay attention to something, you are using your conscious mind. Your subconscious is like the program running in the background that controls most of your body's functions and responses. It processes information from the environment that you aren't paying attention to. It's still recording (even when you are sleeping)—its primary goal being to store and retrieve data—to keep you alive. It controls your autonomic nervous system, which regulates bodily functions like heart rate, blood pressure, and rate of breathing. It's where your long-term memory, beliefs, emotions, and behavior patterns are stored.

I like to refer to the brain as our "supercomputer," because it's like a computer in terms of programming, storage, and retrieval, yet it's more complex, tangled with unpredictable factors. Scientists continue to learn about this vital organ and its interesting abilities to rewire itself. They say, "Neurons that fire together, wire together…." This concept (also known as Hebb's Law) was first introduced in 1949 by Neuropsychologist Donald Hebb in his book *The Organization of Behaviour*.[6] Hebb's Law shows us that every experience, thought or feeling activates thousands of neurons, which form a neural network in the brain. Each time that experience, thought, or feeling is repeated, the brain learns to trigger the same neurons each time. Neural pathways are developed based upon experience and then are automatically recalled by the subconscious mind. Let's dig deeper because this information is key to understanding how your mind and body works.

A computer cannot function without some sort of memory. The same goes for our human brain. For example, learning to tie your shoes, which is taught in kindergarten, can explain the cognitive process of memory. Teachers instruct students how to maneuver the laces by crossing them in a certain way and pulling them through the loop to form a tie. First, children watch the instructor, then try to repeat what they saw. After a few tries, the cognitive thinking process will turn into a memory that's stored in the brain's short-term storage bank. It takes time and practice for every person to accomplish this task. The conscious mind directs the steps as your hands and fingers follow the instructions. It may have been difficult at first, but "practice makes perfect," and you learn how to tie your shoes. Once you repeat the steps several times, this memory is transferred to long-term storage. Your long-term memory allows you to continue a routine without having to think about it. Once you've mastered tying your shoes, you can do it on the fly, while your friends are bugging you to hurry so you can go play. Today, you drive a car, ride a bike, and brush your teeth without ever having to think about how to carry out these activities. Your brain and body are working on autopilot. The subconscious mind achieves it all without thinking.

Think of your conscious mind as the "commander" and the subconscious as the "follower." It's the servant that works 24/7 to ensure you respond in the way you were programmed. The subconscious mind is your program. Motivational speaker and self-development author, Brian Tracy explains:

> *All your habits of thinking and acting are stored in your subconscious mind. It has memorized all your comfort zones and it works to keep you in them... Your subconscious mind causes you to feel emotionally and physically uncomfortable whenever you attempt to do anything new or different or to change any of your established patterns of behavior.*[7]

The past becomes the guidepost for your life experiences. The brain maps everything you are exposed to as a child—it is all downloaded into your subconscious mind. The sounds and signals are picked up by a child's "supercomputer." A child's mind is like a new CPU (Central Processing Unit), ready to be programmed. In psychology, the subconscious is the part of the mind "operating or existing outside of consciousness."[8] It's the part of the mind that stores programming, like a computer's hardware. It processes sensory inputs and experiences into neural networks of synaptic connections. These connections form short-term memory. If you continue to recall that memory or relive that experience, that neural network becomes stronger and turns into a long-term storage file.

Did you know that the average person thinks over 60,000 thoughts daily? Eighty percent are negative; ninety percent are from the past. That means our bodies can believe as if we are living in the past. The subconscious mind is subjective and unable to reason or think independently. It doesn't know the difference between past, present, or future. It's like a computer program running through scenarios or algorithms stored on its hard drive or in a Cloud somewhere. The program running may need to be wiped clean or updated. The communication between your conscious and subconscious mind is critical to overcome limiting beliefs and past trauma—hence the power of repeating mantras or positive affirmations. Without receiving guidance or instruction from your conscious mind, the subconscious will just recall and replay what it knows from your past. It's what makes you feel uncomfortable when presented with an environmental change. The subconscious keeps you stuck in your comfort zone. To improve your results in life is to get in tune with your subconscious mind. Growth occurs when you step outside of your comfort zone. It's imperative for you to understand why your program or mindset may be unconsciously affecting your current way of living. Peel back the layers of conditioning to gain control of your vessel.

Brainwave Frequencies

The human body is a highly complex and interconnected system that uses electrical and chemical signals to carry out its primary functions. Via this amazing machine we call our body, we can think, feel, and act to live our lives and experience our purpose here on Earth. We learn about the basic functions of the body in grade school, but you may not comprehend how significant the power of thought is. When we think, our brain creates a chemical reaction. Neurotransmitters—or your body's chemical messengers—are released, generating an electrical signal in nearby neurons (causing the neurons to fire) and form a thought. The more you repeat a thought, the stronger the connection wired between neurons, forming a neural network. Your central nervous system is made up of vast neural networks and consists of approximately 86 billion neurons that send and receive information between the brain and spinal cord.[9] Dr. James Gordon (founder of the Center for Mind-Body Medicine) says "The brain and peripheral nervous system, the endocrine and immune systems, and indeed, all the organs of our body and all the emotional responses we have, share a common chemical language and are constantly communicating with one another."[10] The subconscious mind controls most of this information, from eating, breathing, digesting, and dreaming to making memories and feeling emotions. What a powerful force—it directs our bodies ninety-five percent of the time without our conscious awareness. Let's dig a little deeper to understand this powerful system and how it takes root in our life.

Doctors and scientists measure brain waves using a technique known as electroencephalography (EEG). Electrodes are placed on a person's head to measure electrical activity or brainwave frequencies. The frequencies (the number of times a wave is repeated in one second) are recorded in hertz. Essentially, this information can rationalize a person's state of consciousness.

Dr. Bruce Lipton explains how children's brains are in download mode from the age of zero to seven. This becomes your screen, the subconscious program that plays on repeat throughout your life, until you become aware of it. Dr. Lipton explains the different levels of consciousness and brain wave frequencies measured by EEG as it relates to children, and says that:

> *For the first six years of a child's life, the conscious part of the brain is not primarily functioning. The brain is functioning at a very low EEG level, called theta. A child is observing the environment just like a television camera, recording everything, bypassing consciousness—which isn't working yet—and going straight into the subconscious. The child uses its parents as the teachers to fill in the data in the subconscious mind.*[11]

What a child observes, hears, and experiences up until seven years of age is not only out of their control but is programmed as information their subconscious mind will reference from then on. Most people can't recall many memories from birth to five years of age—unless there was a significant emotional response attached to that memory. Nonetheless, our subconscious remembers everything.

*The following image identifies the different brain wave frequencies.

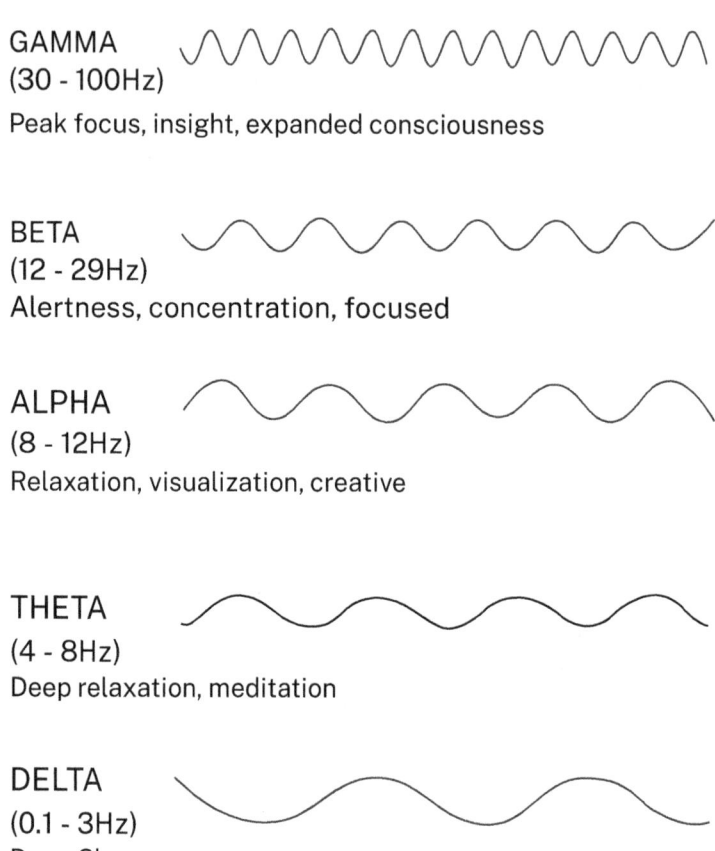

GAMMA
(30 - 100Hz)
Peak focus, insight, expanded consciousness

BETA
(12 - 29Hz)
Alertness, concentration, focused

ALPHA
(8 - 12Hz)
Relaxation, visualization, creative

THETA
(4 - 8Hz)
Deep relaxation, meditation

DELTA
(0.1 - 3Hz)
Deep Sleep

These frequencies are levels of awareness in the brain. From conception to age one, a baby's brain is operating in the slowest frequency known as Delta Waves (0.1-3 Hz). This is the highest form of receptivity and a mental state associated with deep sleep. It makes sense since infants sleep a lot during their first year. Delta waves show up in stage 3 and 4 of our sleep cycles and stimulate healing and regeneration.[12] As babies transition into a toddler, from ages two- to six-years-old, their brain waves shift to the Theta level (4-8 Hz). We associate this brainwave frequency with states of hypnosis where information can be downloaded into the subconscious mind. Think about it. Babies learn and accomplish more in the first two years of life than at any other time. The brain is downloading every single piece of information it's introduced to. They learn to eat, crawl, walk, talk, follow directions, get dressed, play games and so on. Theta is a state where imagination and reality can blend into one. For example, when I was six years old, my imaginary friends were real to me. Lisa was my best friend. Kids have vivid imaginations; they live on a different level of awareness than adults do. That carpet is a magic carpet to them. Life has not yet conditioned them to believe otherwise. However, whatever they are introduced to during these innocent years of growth will become their conditioning later on. In my opinion, this is the most important fact to understand as a parent.

During this time of my life, my parents fought. My sister called me names and made fun of me often. At a young age, my subconscious downloaded criticism, separation, and verbal abuse. It's interesting that we are not in control during the time we are downloading the program that will run our adult life. You may not make decisions for yourself until you turn eighteen. During your growing years, while your program is being inherited, you are subject to the rules, biases, and expectations of your caretakers and social systems. Sometimes, these impositions do not serve the greater good for your life. They are serving someone else's larger agenda and are part of a larger (often faulty) program. The way your parents behave has a direct influence on your behavior. The environment—people, places, and things you are exposed to—has an impact on who you become. Your subconscious mind stores the programming.

As an adult, Theta can be accessed through meditation or if you are in a sleepy or drowsy state. If you have practiced meditation, you know how a deep state of relaxation that is unconnected to your external environment feels. This level allows for vivid imagination and the opportunity to access your intuition—the invisible yet powerful insight from a higher power.

Children transition into higher states of consciousness—Alpha (8-12 Hz) from six to twelve years of age, and then Beta (above 12 Hz) after twelve. As adults, we typically operate at the Alpha and Beta frequency levels. Alpha is like a resting state for the brain or level of awareness when you are present in the moment. "Alpha waves aid overall mental co-ordination, calmness and alertness, mind/body integration and learning."[13] Beta waves are found in normal waking states of consciousness when your mind is directed towards a mental activity like decision-making or problem-solving. The highest brainwave frequency is known as Gamma (it oscillates between 30-100 Hz), which is a state of heightened perception and peak performance. This state of consciousness has attracted researchers to explore further its restorative powers.

Can you see now just how powerful our mind is? Our ability to target certain states of consciousness can have a profound impact on the way we live our lives. Whatever programming you picked up as a child has a direct effect on your behavior as an adult—but only if you allow it. Rest assured; it doesn't have to be your final story or follow you for the rest of your life (if you don't want it to).

Mass Programming

You see, awareness gives you power, but most people don't realize the program exists. Even worse, they don't know that we live in a quantum, ever-expanding universe where all possibilities exist. The act of observing collapses waves of probability into particles of creation. You influence the world around you and the environment has an influence on you. Anything you observe, you give power to. You are a Quantum (a part of the whole quantum universe) in which everything is connected. We just view it as separate. Thoughts and feelings are energy—everything is energy.

It's all connected, yet people are separated by borders, ethnicity, gender, religion, and classifications. They are divided by money and the systems it funds. The belief is taught and passed down from generation to generation. It is the screen through which we view our world. You inherit the box in grade school, the school system puts you into classifications, and your family programs your way of thinking about yourself and others.

Our brains are like supercomputers, yet we don't know how to harness ninety-five percent of their infinite and innate capacity. What we learn, experience, and endure as children through adolescence into early adulthood becomes our program. We are taught our limitations. In school, they didn't teach us about the power of our mind, the electromagnetic harmony of our hearts, or that we are energy beings capable of co-creating our reality. They did not teach us that Universal Laws—like the Law of Attraction and the Law of Resonance—govern all things. We can attract opportunities and certain people into our life by harmonizing our mind and body to certain vibrational frequencies. We can reprogram our subconscious mind!

Science is catching up to clarify the invisible miracles that spirituality and religions have referenced for millennia. The problem is, these scientific breakthroughs are not broadcast on the Nightly News. Our education system does not teach our kids they can do anything they put their minds to. In fact, children hear the word "No" more times than any other word until they become conditioned and trained in their way of thinking, feeling, and acting. "No, you cannot do that! Do it this way. Stop laughing, talking, and running around having fun! Sit still and be quiet!" Our society has been built upon a system that is failing.

The Industrial Revolution began the indoctrination of conformity at school. We train children to walk in line, raise their hands to speak, and to not bring attention to themselves. We tell them to just listen and follow the rules. Society prepares children to become factory workers. We teach separation, racism, and conformity. What if those rules are outdated? What if they do not serve a child's personal or social development? What if a child is a born entrepreneur or engineer who sees past the limitations imposed on everyone? Society has led us to believe in a way of living that serves someone else's agenda and may not be serving our purpose on this planet.

Our species and this planet are changing by orders of magnitude, but the direction we are taking may not be the best route. World wars, technological revolutions, how we travel, communicate, educate, and vaccinate has shifted our realities in more ways than you can fathom. We are witnessing profound changes in human history. Our world is not the same as it used to be 100 years ago. Nikola Tesla and Albert Einstein understood and communicated the fundamentals of the universe in the early 1900s, but today, most people still don't comprehend that energy, vibration, and frequency are at the root of life. It's a mystery to some (and seems impossible to others), but like I said, science is beginning to prove what ancient indigenous cultures and philosophers have been telling stories about for centuries. If you search for the information, it's there, but "they" don't broadcast this powerful knowledge to the masses. Imagine how that would affect the powerful people reaping the benefits of your suffering. Pharmaceutical companies, governments, banks, insurance companies, tech giants—they are cashing in on your need for more while meditating in the Mediterranean.

Society is fixated on acquiring more money and fame. People have been brainwashed; tricked into believing in a particular reality, as it's playing like a fiddle on the news. Television. That was the first mistake. "Welcome to this regularly scheduled programming." A new era of illusions introduced in the 1950s. ABC, CBS, NBC. Do you see? Mass programming. A way to communicate information through television, radio, publishing, and the internet. Who owns the media we see today?

"In 1983, the largest 50 corporations controlled ninety percent of the media. Today, because of massive mergers and takeovers, six corporations control ninety percent of what we see, hear, and read...These powerful corporations also have an agenda, and it would be naïve not to believe that their views and needs impact coverage of issues important to them." [14]
—Bernie Sanders, 2017

What is important to them? More money. More opportunity. More people who need their solutions. People who don't see the truth. They don't seek the truth; they just follow the leader. The first recognizable social media site, Six Degrees, was created in 1997. Since then, our society has progressed into a social media and screen addiction where our time is consumed by everything electronic. Cell phones, computers, iPads, TV screens, app notifications—we are plugged into information, images, and sounds all the time. Instant gratification, observation, and interaction. When was the last time you spent a full day in nature without a device?

Kids who play video games are living in a simulation. Take Fortnite, for example. It's a virtual reality world created from someone's clever idea—350 million people play it for an average of six to ten hours a day.[15] This game takes on a reality of its own in the minds of our children. They become a part of the simulation. They reemphasize that reality by watching YouTube of other kids playing and talking about Fortnite. This pastime (and others like it) is shifting our consciousness on our planet. It distracts us, moves us from focusing on the physical world to concentrating on a fake world.

The same goes for social media. People scroll through filtered pictures, edited videos, and over-emphasized celebrations which shift our perception of the people and world around us. You may look at a post and see a picture-perfect family, but *behind the screen*, they are far from perfect. Maybe they had a big fight right before the photographer shot that photo of their fake smiles. Maybe there is a broken heart and a depressed soul behind that person's smiling face. Perhaps underneath that shiny diamond wedding ring is a woman who is abused, taken for granted, or feels empty. Possibly behind that million-dollar home is a family who doesn't talk, has no connection, and whose children yearn for love. We are becoming a lost species, distracted by perceptions and reflections of a simulated reality.

This trillion-dollar industry is designed to suck you into the simulation. Apple, Microsoft, Alphabet (Google), and Amazon have managed to achieve $1 trillion or more in market capitalization.[16] These big tech companies have become extremely powerful, enabling the elite to make decisions on behalf of humanity behind the scenes, without our knowledge or approval. We have become so dependent on the virtual world they control. They can influence your behavior and direct your attention for their own benefit. Every screen you view is part of this matrix of corruption that evolves with every new viewer. Every new like, subscription, and comment energizes the beast of separation. Is it out of control? When will the truth be revealed?

Oil has always been the world's most valuable resource—but data surpassed oil in 2019. The new commodity on this planet now is—YOU! Your data. It's recorded, sold, and used to persuade you for the benefit of someone else's agenda. Facebook, Google, Instagram, and many other companies collect your personal data, including facial recognition, voice data, and object recognition, to cater to your needs. There are data brokers who market your personality to other companies who pay for ads to target you. You are a target. Are you conscious of this ploy to gain your attention or feed your distraction? Do you see how we have lost our power in this technological revolution of capitalism? Will we wake up? Or will the bright lights and fake fame continue to hypnotize humankind?

Our children are growing up in this altered state of consciousness. They are inheriting this program. It's a fractal. It keeps repeating and developing like numbers do—infinitely. (We'll talk more about fractals in Chapter 7). When will we wake up to the fact that our power is being depleted, our rights are being ripped away, and our hearts are not in harmony? The news is depressing, programmed to fuel our minds with fear and worry. That fear feeds our bodies with dangerous hormones and chemical reactions that inhibit our health and happiness. We are viewing our outer environment through a fictitious lens. This egoic lens is founded by fear, funded by the beast of corruption.

The United States of America has always been known as the land of the free. "Let freedom ring" as we celebrate our independence and civil liberties. This is no longer the case in America today. Are we living within another simulation? Society has trained us to believe that our healthcare system helps us, our financial system is there to support us, and our educational system is the best way to teach our children how to be the best they can be. It has indoctrinated us into believing that this is the best way of living. Take this pill for your symptom and it will solve the problem. Listen to your teachers, they know everything. Don't argue with adults. Get a credit card to improve your credit score. Invest in the stock market with the hard-earned money you sacrificed time with your family for. Go to church to be saved. You need to have a college degree to be successful. Wear the mask to reduce the spread. Get the vaccine or lose your job. How did we get here? It's like our country is burning in flames of fury before our eyes.

Stop. Drop and Roll. In elementary school, we learned this simple technique to survive a fire. Maybe they should have taught us about meditation and focused breathing to help with our anxiety and depression. What about social media comparison syndrome and bullying? Is there a high school curriculum developed to teach students how to deal with their emotions, overactive mind, obsessive thoughts, fear, anxiety, shame, unhappiness, or anger? Why do we focus on politics, war, and fighting more than on healing our internal wounds? Are we overlooking the critical elements that deplete our power because the program distracts us? Are we stuck in the matrix? What is the ultimate agenda—of our government? Our education system? Our healthcare system? Our financial institutions? What is the ultimate agenda within each family unit? Where does the program **begin and end**?

Chapter 3
A System of Transformation

Awareness

> "Awareness is all about restoring your freedom to choose what you want instead of what your past imposes on you." [17]
> —Deepak Chopra

One word. One act. One focus. It seems so simple, yet most people are unaware. Awareness is the key to evolution, consciousness, and change. Change must begin with you. The only person you can change is you. Your state of being—your energy, vibration, and frequency—are superpowers you can harness through awareness that your thoughts create the feelings in your body, and they in turn drive your actions. Your actions create your results and affect the people around you. We live in a dual reality—mental and physical interactions influence each other. You and I are products of the interactions within our environments. The famous paraphrased quote "As above, so below"[18] comes from the second verse of the *Emerald Tablet* of Hermes Trismegistus. It provides profound insight that we exist on a spiritual and physical plane. There are many interpretations of meaning and various versions of this powerful quote that summarize the relationship between the macrocosm and microcosm. *The Kybalion*, a book published by Three Initiates in 1908, explains seven Hermetic principles:

> "As above, so below; as below, so above." [...] This Principle is of universal application and manifestation, on the various planes of the material, mental, and spiritual universe- it is an Universal Law. [...] Just as a knowledge of the Principles of Geometry enables man to measure distant suns and their movements, while seated in his observatory, so a knowledge of the Principle of Corre-

A SYSTEM OF TRANSFORMATION

spondence enables Man to reason intelligently from the Known to the Unknown.[19]

If you want to change the results in your life, you must start by raising your level of awareness and consciousness. Realize your true power and learn the Universal Laws of life so you can apply them to transform spiritually. When you do, you impact the whole (the world around you—Universe at large). Increase your awareness to the effects of your choices: Who you surround yourself with, the foods you eat, your social media engagement, how you decide to carry out your daily activities—these decisions turn into your week-long progress. Weeks add up to years and ultimately become your *Life Timeline*. Your choices determine the results of your life just like every cause has an effect within the Universe. Once you increase your awareness then your actions will determine your course. It is time for you to take control of your life and adopt a positive worldview, so you can influence the people around you and the world as a whole.

I want to see our children's generation rise above the egoic mindset and get back to the basics of life. I pray they will realize their power, use it for good, and rise above limitation and separation to join energetic forces and overcome the screens of ill will, hatred, and judgment. It's time for us to realize our infinite potential and our connection to Source. The power that breathes our bodies every second of every day is almighty and untapped.

You are a product of creation, and you are a creator. We are all creators because we are all observers. The Universe is alive. You are it. I am YOU. We are one, and we hold the Power. Most are just UNAWARE.

It's time to **CONNECT TO YOUR POWER** and raise your awareness. The present moment is "the present"—it's the gift of life. Through your consciousness, you can make the world a better place in many ways.

This is no longer my story. Holding on to memories reinforces the emptiness I felt for years. Instead of dealing with or processing the pain and hurt that flooded my being over twenty years ago, I built walls of steel around my heart and tried to turn off all feeling. I wanted to feel numb. I shut down and ran away from my problems. Cutting my heart chakra off from the world, I went dark and lost connection with my spirit. I became a runner! Others may have viewed me as a screen of strength (strong and independent) when inside, I was weak and lonely.

You can never know what someone is hiding behind their screen. Behind that bully's intimidating character could be a child who was severely abused; behind that celebrity's infamous lifestyle could be a person who struggles with anxiety and depression; behind that handshake could be a dirty deal; behind that handsome man's smile or charismatic character could be a narcissistic liar and cheat. Who are we to judge anyone else? I believe that judgement is merely a reflection that mirrors some sort of truth (behind your screen). If you don't have a reason to judge, why would you?

Many people struggle with self-love and self-acceptance. Often, they feel unworthy of true happiness because they believe they are not good enough, pretty enough, or smart enough. I know because I have dealt with that unruly voice in my head, reassuring me of my shortcomings and insecurities. Are you on the sidelines, not engaging in life because of incessant self-doubt? Are you struggling with others' judgment or the criticism that lives in your subconscious mind, reminding you every day of your faults? Are you repeating self-sabotaging patterns that affect your family or relationships? Have you tried to escape from heartbreak that turned into addiction? These programs play out *behind the screen* of many people's lives. Those experiences have constructed their *Life Timelines*, and affect their health, wellbeing, relationships, and career progression. We don't know a lot about another person's screen. For me, for example, while others saw me as strong and resilient, for half my life, I struggled. Judgment, ridicule, depression, anxiety, and self-conscious thoughts plagued my teenage life. I fell in love with a man who broke my heart more times than I can count. I dealt with racism and abandonment. I cried myself to sleep on countless nights and attempted suicide more than once. We struggle with these problems alone and often search for an escape to numb the pain. We resort to drugs, alcohol, sex, food or some other form of escape. Over time, these stimuli become our habits. Our monkey mind runs the show.

Who is directing your screen show? Is it your conscious awareness, connected to intention? Or is it your needy, egoic, unfulfilled program influenced by the voids of your past? Think about this. Take your "self" out of the picture. View your screen from an outsider's perspective. What do you see? This is indicative of the facts. Your intuition is always pointing in the right direction. Overrule the monkey mind by connecting back to Source. What are you longing for?

It's impossible to correct a problem when you don't understand the underlying root cause of the issue. How do you solve problems? The first step is to become aware you have a problem. Then, make the choice to TAG IT! Point it out. Observe it for what it is. Is it a behavior, habit, or pattern that does not serve you or those around you? Your first step is AWARENESS. Once you know you have an issue to solve, you can apply the *7-Step Life Timeline System of Transformation*.

The 7-Step Life Timeline System of Transformation

For the past fifteen years, I have studied personal development and learned strategies to overcome my programmed way of thinking. During this introspective journey, I developed a way to transform my life using this 7-Step system. As noted earlier, I remove my mask and reveal painful experiences, perceptions, and subconscious programming—all to show you the effectiveness of this system.

I reflect on my *Life Timeline* by tagging certain patterns of behavior I exhibited for years—until I became curious and conscious of the fact that I was repeating self-defeating habits. I hope you will see my perspective of the *Life Timeline* from zero to forty years linearly from the memories I share. For example, I often told men I liked that they should "lose my phone number." I realized that this unconscious switch was a defense mechanism I used to protect myself from getting hurt—again. I was holding on to the notion of a "broken family" and isolating myself from people who loved me—but that just kept me facing a lack of love.

I learned to tag instinctive reactions in real-time, then apply steps to override that behavior—and you can, too. In the present, you will identify the recurring pattern(s) or ways of thinking that are not serving your passion or purpose. You will learn how to apply the *7-Step Life TimeLine System of Transformation* to your life. Ready? After an overview, we will dive deeper into each step as we move through the book.

A SYSTEM OF TRANSFORMATION

Step 1 – TAG IT:

Pay attention to your way of thinking or notice what you are noticing. Become the observer of your thoughts and feelings without engaging. Just notice—the way you react to people, the obsessive thoughts in your head, the worry or doubt you feel. Notice them all... in present moments. Pay attention to repeating behaviors or reactions. Don't judge them or yourself. Just notice. You can detach from that behavior through your awareness. TAG IT. That is the first step. Observe the behavior, way of thinking, or unconscious reaction without engaging in the feeling. Notice it. TAG IT.

Write it down and pin it up on your *Life Timeline*, the day you "tagged it."

MY LIFE TIMELINE
Write it down and pin it up on your Life Timeline, the day you "tagged it."

BEHIND THE SCREEN

MY LIFE TIMELINE
Write it down and pin it up on your Life Timeline, the day you "tagged it."

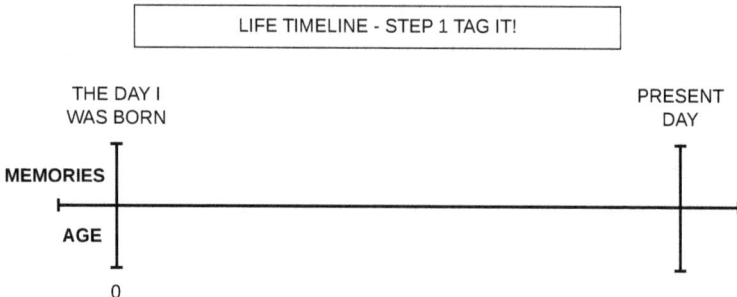

Step 2 – REMEMBER IT:

Take a moment to remember the first time you experienced something like this—that way of thinking or feeling. Go back to the beginning. The program's download is strongest between zero to seven years old, remember? Just remember the first time. Once you get to that long-term memory storage compartment, try to recall that memory and all its details. Pin each memory (that repeats the same story) up on your *Life Timeline* at the age you experienced it.

MY LIFE TIMELINE
After applying Step 1 - TAG IT (your issue), list the first memory of this experience and your age.

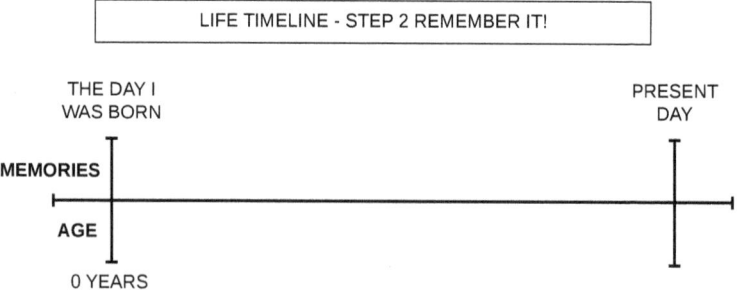

A SYSTEM OF TRANSFORMATION

For example, during my *Life Timeline*, my parents divorced when I was eight. That was the first time I felt separation and heartache. I was part of a broken family. Later, I attracted a man who broke my heart for the next nine years (age fourteen to twenty-three). At twenty-six, another man broke my heart and replayed the notion of a broken family. When I was thirty-three, another man broke my heart, and another at thirty-eight. Do you see the pattern? It seemed like any man I cared about ended up hurting me, so my program got stuck on FLIGHT and separation. Run... Don't get hurt... Don't trust... Don't believe him... He's going to screw you over. Any time I opened up, gave my love, or allowed myself to be vulnerable, others took advantage of me.

These subconscious feelings triggered—or created—my reactions.

MY LIFE TIMELINE

After applying Step 1 - TAG IT (Fear of Heart Break / Broken Family), list the first memory of this experience and your age. If you experienced this issue multiple times, list each memory and age.

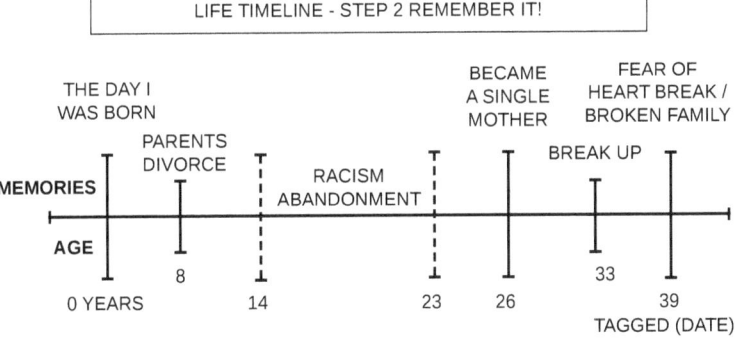

Step 3 – FEEL IT:

Now that you have tapped into the first memory of this (and the several instances that followed), feel into how you felt then. Allow yourself to feel that emotion, NOW. This is where we get blocked energetically. Instead of dealing with pain, loss, or resentment, we bottle up those emotions and drown them with alcohol, drugs, or something else. We run away and don't look back. The problem is that energy doesn't get destroyed. You can't run from energy or emotions because they are energy in motion. If you bottle them up, that energy gets stuck. It plagues you by lowering your vibrational frequency and forcing you to repeat the scenario until you get sick of the same results. That's when you are ready to find the solution. The solution is releasing those feelings. Letting them go. But you can't do that until you have processed them in the way they needed to be processed. You have to work hard now. Feel those emotions like you should have felt them back then. Allow yourself the opportunity to feel.

This may not be easy, but it is worthwhile. If you went through traumatizing pain, you will need professional support during this process.

Step 4 – FLIP IT:

We are wired to focus only on negative memories and emotions like hurt or pain. The next step will challenge you to flip it; shift your perspective and try to look through the screen from a different angle. What good could have resulted from the situation? Try to remember the other side the ego hides from in the shadows. Focus on that good and feel it even in the smallest sense. Look for the silver lining in any way, shape, or form.

Step 5 – RELEASE IT:

This is where the process gets fun. Release it! Let that compartmentalized energy go now. You have uncovered the memories and emotions from the past. Now you release that energy to be recycled into the Universe. Let go and let God (or whatever higher power you believe in) expel the energy and its bonds from your being.

Step 6 – REPROGRAM:

Allow your brain to do what it does best, wire synaptic connections. You've released that past energy. Now you can envision a new story, a fulfilling screen to see, feel, and live by. Be descriptive as you envision your future so the Universe can deliver all the details you deserve. You can create a new program that is empowering, loving, and fulfilling. Form a crystal-clear picture in your mind of your dream life and play it like a movie on your screen. Keep it playing. You are building a short-term memory into a long-term program. The key is to put the HOW on hold. Your monkey mind will attempt to ruin your dream. Don't allow it to make your limitations more visible than your purpose. The Universe works in abundant ways. You don't need to know how your vision will come to fruition; you just need to see it. Then move on to the next step!

Step 7 – RESONATE:

As you envision living the life of your dreams, while believing in the transformation taking place in your life, you MUST feel like the person who is experiencing that way of thinking and feeling—NOW. You become what you believe, but more importantly, what you feel. Resonate with that harmonic frequency in your physical feeling body. We exist energetically on a physical and spiritual plane connected by subatomic particles that are always vibrating. Align with that infinite, omnipresent "Quantum Field" of energy. Believe and feel yourself living

BEHIND THE SCREEN

from that viewpoint. Feel healed, feel loved, feel the freedom you deserve.

Speak it. Feel it. Act on it. Become it. Use my mantra by repeating, "I can, I will, I am."

Rinse and Repeat!

THE LIFE TIMELINE IS LIKE A CLOTHESLINE
Clothes are like the memories pinned up at the age they were experienced.

| Carrie's Life Timeline Example |

MEMORIES

TAG IT!
FEAR OF HEARTBREAK / BROKEN FAMILY

PARENTS DIVORCE — RACISM — ABANDONMENT — SINGLE MOTHER

AGE 8   14   15   26   39

Imagine your *Life Timeline* like a clothesline. It's kind of like hanging your clothes out to dry. As you tag a behavior, identify it on your *Life Timeline* (today). Remember the age at which you were first introduced to that type of behavior and mark it on the *Life Timeline* (at that age). Since the program has been on repeat for years, you may recall several memories reflecting that same behavior. If so, mark each memory at the age of inception on your *Life Timeline*. You may be attracting the same circumstances unconsciously and replaying the same responses repeatedly. So, every time you TAG IT, rinse and repeat the steps while you map them on the *Life Timeline*. It should be used as a tool to see the chronological events of your life and understand why you may repeat certain patterns of behavior unconsciously, contributing to the story being replayed. If you take this system seriously, you will begin to see the screen in so many ways.

The 21/90 Rule

The 21/90 Rule states: It takes twenty-one days to make a habit and ninety days to make a permanent lifestyle change. Continue these steps for the next ninety days. If your download took place over twenty years ago, it's going to take time to reprogram a new way of thinking and being. Remember, you have a powerful supercomputer in our head (protected by a thick skull) that sends signals through your central nervous system to operate your body. Those signals are nothing more than chemical reactions and hormones being released to instruct your body on how to behave. That's why we call them "behaviors." Your body operates within an environment based on its programming. As we talked about earlier, that program was probably installed against your knowledge in circumstances that were out of your control. Most of these programs are faulty, unnecessary for survival, yet our bodies operate according to survival of the fittest. They always have—the fight-or-flight response was necessary for humans to survive hundreds of years ago, but today, it's not serving us.

Instead of being chased by a bear today, people are rushing around, dwelling on their problems, distracted by negative news, living in a state of stress. Stress kills! Awareness coupled with action is critical to reverse the train. Stop fight-or-flight in its tracks: Tag it, Remember it, Feel it, Flip it, Release it, Reprogram, Resonate, Rinse and Repeat. It all starts with awareness. One word. One action. One focus. Focus on your way of thinking, notice every emotion you feel and connect to its source. Apply the seven steps to overcome your subconscious programming, break through that screen and **transform your life.**

Chapter 4
The Download

Childhood Innocence

"What we are today comes from our thoughts of yesterday, and our present thoughts build our life of tomorrow: Our life is the creation of our mind." [20]
—Gautama Buddha

I **relied on Lisa.** Like a friendly guardian angel, she was there for me anytime. "It's OK, Carrie," she'd say, "just smell the flowers." I talked to Lisa often, most of the time. She was my sidekick. When I was a child, she coached me through my parents' arguments. Dad slammed doors often and that made me tremble. Lisa consoled me. Trying to direct my attention to the positive aspects of life, she was a sound voice and trusted friend. We played house, Life, Barbie's, Operation, school, and basketball together. We laughed, and we argued. We explored the woods, played in the back yard, and rode bikes through the neighborhood, talking and laughing. No matter what, she was always there when I needed someone to talk to. Later, Vicki and Stacey joined the crew. They introduced some drama, but it was all good fun. We explored many dimensions in those young learning years. Carrie, Vicki, Lisa, and Stacey—my three imaginary friends! They helped me when I felt scared and alone. My parents fought often, so I called on them to comfort me and keep me from feeling alone.

My Dad called me "Poke," like the Pokey Little Puppy because I used to poke along. Mom called me "Carebear," while my sister, Kim, called me "Pee-Pee Baby" and tortured me like typical older siblings do. Kim was an only child until I came along when she was eight and stole her thunder. She made me pay for that, but still, I idolized her. My father was a baker and made barely enough money to get by. Like most women in the

1980s, my mother was a "stay at home mom." I can remember waking up early, grabbing a jar of peanut butter and a spoon, then sitting on the couch to watch cartoons like *The Care Bears* and *Fraggle Rock*. I loved *Fraggle Rock*! Kim would be getting ready for school—she would tease her hair and spray her bangs with Aqua Net until they were at a perfect peak on top of her forehead. She was so cool! At every opportunity, I followed Kim and her friends around. I felt like one special kid when I could hang out with them.

My best friend, Ashley, and I would play cops and robbers around the neighborhood. I was the leader and enjoyed coming up with new games and ways to make money. (I was always an entrepreneur at heart). Ashley and I sold lemonade, iced tea, bracelets we handcrafted, even pictures we drew. We spent our summer days catching crayfish down by the creek. We played outside until the streetlights came on. Those were the good old days, when kids lived outside and we used our imaginations to create things to do with our time, like making mud pies or clearing trails to ride through the woods on our bikes. We also used to sit on her front porch eating bologna and mustard sandwiches, studying the *Encyclopedia Britannica*, teaching our imaginary classroom of students. These were great childhood memories. We hardly ever wanted to be in the house—until Super Mario Brothers and Nintendo came out, that is. That's when the video game and screen addiction began.

As with anything good, there comes some bad. My dark and scary memories came from my dad screaming at my mother. This started when I was six or seven years old. Due to my mother's decision to get a job, my father accused her of cheating with her boss and called her a "whore." She wasn't allowed to wear skirts to work, and the tension continued to build in our household. I recall constant fighting, yelling, doors slamming. My Dad's voice was so loud, it scared me and made my stomach bunch into tight knots. My sister felt bad for me, so she told me to hide in her room and turn up the radio. I'd put a cassette tape in the boombox and turn up the music to drown out the yelling. KISS, Ozzy Osbourne, Hank Williams Jr., and Poison were my go-to tunes. I would lie in Kim's bed and cry, feeling alone and unstable.

Maybe your parents went through a divorce when you were a child? Possibly, you are an adult who went through a divorce yourself. Sadly, the effects of this can have a lasting impact on many lives. Did you know that nowadays, over fifty percent of marriages in the U.S. end in divorce? God assigned me to share what divorce looks like to a child *Behind My Screen*.

When I was eight years old, my parents sat me down at the kitchen table one evening and broke the news. They were getting a divorce. I would move out of my house into an apartment with my mom and start a new life in a new school district. My sister would stay with my dad. What is an eight-year-old to make of this? It made me nervous. I got belly aches a lot. Anxiety and adrenaline from the fight-or-flight response took root in my being. The only good thing was that our apartment was down the street from my best friend Ashley's house—her family lived next door to my maternal grandmother, Grandma Madden. I called her Gram. It's difficult when families separate, especially for children, and looking back, I see the impact it had on me. At this time in my *Life Timeline*, my hardware program was being installed. Then it became a subconscious mental program which stuck with me for years.

Even though I idolized my sister, she couldn't stand me. She tormented me and made fun of me, calling me names like "Mosquito Bites," and "eight-year-old genius," because my breasts weren't developed yet and I asked a lot of questions. Until I was about twelve, she picked on me all the time.

I internalized her words and negative remarks. Her criticizing behavior turned into my self-judgment. I felt powerless, alone, and unloved. The download continued. It's never intentional, is it? We are just unaware that it's happening.

Can you relate to stories of conflict, shame, or fear you experienced as a child? How did your story develop? Often, to avoid feeling the negative emotions they cause, we store these files deep in our psyche. The problem is, they don't go away. As we grow up, they turn into unconscious triggers and reactive behavioral patterns we use to cope with reality. Children are vulnerable to what their program becomes. Parents can repeat their own childhood programming. Their reactions to certain triggers, their gained behaviors and patterns of suffering are passed down to their children unconsciously. The child experiences the effects of their parents' program, and the cycle continues. None of us really heal from these wounds. Why? Because we are unaware of the subconscious programming, its impact on our lives, or how to deal with the pain from the past. What if we could learn to overcome the painful programs installed in our early years and reprogram our mind and body with positive and loving self-fulfilling prophecies?

> *"The visions we offer our children shape the future.*
> *It matters what those visions are.*
> *Often they become self-fulfilling prophecies.*
> *Dreams are maps."* [21]
> —Carl Sagan

A Broken Family

A self-fulfilling prophecy is like the placebo effect. In other words, what you believe will most likely manifest. Maybe it's because what we believe affects the way we act. It signals certain feelings or e-motions. All our e-motions are energy in motion. They influence our actions. If e-motions are not properly processed, then they turn into suppressed negative energy hidden within the invisible realm that will follow you throughout life. It's present even if you don't realize it, because we cannot create or destroy energy. Energy can only be transformed.

Releasing constricted energy isn't easy. This book represents a progression of release for me... remembering experiences from my childhood that shaped my character, allowing myself to feel the emotions from difficult events, flipping the story to see another point of view, and releasing stuck energy to co-create a new way of being inspired me to originate the *Life Timeline System of Transformation*. It takes time and practice for anyone to reprogram their way of living, but it is worth the effort.

Today, I make every effort to live my life according to the principles shared in this book. Present moment awareness and intentionality help me navigate through life. The present moment is your opportunity to be conscious, to see the truth. Time is an illusion, a series of present moments. You make decisions within each moment that influence the course of your *Life Timeline*. I decided it was important to write this book, to share the truth "behind my screen," so that readers will have more awareness and power than they did before.

We paint the pictures of our life on our own internal screen. These pictures shift overtime. The stories we tell of our memories change based on our state of being at the time we recall each memory. Studies show that a large percent of our memories of the past are not always true. Yet, we spend a great deal of our lifetimes thinking about past situations and circumstances, allowing them to play on our current screen. So, what's playing on your screen may not be accurate, may not be serving you and your family, may restrict your energy body, and may inhibit you from living the life you yearn for.

As an example, I recall a memory from my past that no longer serves me. One weekend, when I was eight, I was staying at my dad's house and my sister was watching me because Dad had gone out. In the middle of the night, I was asleep in my dad's bed (in my parent's old bedroom) when I was awakened by Dad yelling. Doors slammed. My body shut down. I lay there, terrified. What was happening? Why was he so mad? The room was dark. The bedroom door was cracked open. My sister turned on the hallway light. The light and my sister's presence gave me a bit of comfort. I could see Dad in the hallway, yelling, telling my sister what had happened. His voice was filled with anger, pain, resentment—and a hint of pride. I caught pieces of the story, and all the while, my stomach bunched into knots, my blood pumped through my veins, and my body shook with fear. Dad slandered Mom, called her a whore. He'd caught her at a local bar with a man. He'd keyed her car, then followed them back to "our" new apartment. I guess she'd invited the man back to hang out. My Dad walked into her kitchen screaming, "You are not going to fuck my wife!" The man tried to hide in the pantry. Dad grabbed him and shoved him through the drywall. I wasn't old enough to understand the complexity of the situation, but looking back now, I realize that my sister and I, at sixteen and eight, absorbed all that negative energy, drama, and projected pain. Imagine how I felt the next day when Mom came to pick me up—there was silence on our drive home. The energy was cold and lonely.

We pulled off the freeway into the driveway and walked toward our new apartment, which did not feel like home at all. It was small and cold in every room. We used to heat the kitchen with the electric oven door open—we had electric baseboard heat and it was too expensive to turn on. We were so poor; we ate tuna salad sandwiches and canned soup a few times a week because it was cheap and easy to make.

    I walked up the stairs, removed my shoes in the hallway, and walked into the large yellow kitchen. I opened the pantry door. There, carved into the drywall, was the silhouette of a man. That silhouette remained for the three years we lived there. Every time I opened the pantry to get cereal, I was reminded of that little girl, alone in the dark, scared, playing out the drama of these stories in her head. That moment played on repeat every weekend she traveled between her parents' homes, back and forth between the hate and resentment, between environments of pain, despair, poverty, and loneliness, and the energy of a broken home. Her family would never be complete again. This memory—and feelings like this—downloaded into my subconscious mind as a program. "A Broken Family." This story still plays through my screen today.

    The five years that followed were difficult. Every weekend, I had to pack up my things, go to a different house with a different lifestyle and try to play with a different set of friends. Later, Dad sold the house and rented an apartment. I lost all sense of stability. TAG IT, REMEMBER IT, FEEL IT… I felt lost and lonely, as if they were forcing me to live someone else's life. My mother started dating, and that was hard for me to accept and endure. I hated the men she dated. Dad resented my mother. In fact, he was disgusted by her and he let everyone know it. Dad called Mom terrible names. He wouldn't speak to her, look at her, or even be in the same room as her. My sister and my father would talk derogatorily about Mom. It made me feel small. Sick in the pit of my stomach.

    Resentment can eat a person—and a family—alive. My father resented my mother for over twenty years. I became a confused nine- to ten-year-old. I was trying to fit into a new school, make new friends. It was hard. I came home from school every day and ate a bag of chips and dip. I put on weight. My mom told me I was getting fat. Her remarks made me feel worse. She made me sick, too. My grandmother and aunts would talk about Mom behind her back, because she would leave me with them or with my sister and go out with her boyfriends. She changed her likes and hobbies with every new man. For the rest of my childhood, I was stuck between negative energy and ridicule. I heard everything derogatory everyone said about my mother, and I internalized it all. This became my download—a screen I still looked through as an adult.

Through writing down my stories, I realized *I can change this*. I can apply Step 1 – TAG IT. I realize I've had an unconscious resentment towards my mother for a long time. I became aware of my thoughts and feelings when she came around. I started to notice the way I would react to certain things she said or did. She would talk or complain about other people or tell me what to do—and that would set me off. I used this system to TAG my reoccurring behavior patterns (the way I reacted to my mother) and try to identify why they have continued for so long. It's like I carry around a remaining layer of disgust left over from my father and sister (my sister hasn't spoken to Mom in several years). I feel like sometimes Mom lives in her own world and doesn't see how she projects her issues onto others. I can see my sister's and father's perspectives and that viewpoint has impacted my relationship with my mother. I don't like to see through this lens, but oftentimes my response is an unconscious, automatic reaction. I react by getting an attitude with her, yelling, or trying to avoid her and then afterward she makes me feel bad—or I automatically feel bad. It's a heavy burden I've been carrying around for twenty-eight years! The reflections and projections can run deep. It will take dedicated mental work and energy to apply the seven steps to my *Life Timeline* to override this way of thinking about and feeling towards my mother. I've identified the triggers that I react to today (TAG), then I went back and recalled (REMEMBER) the onset of those types of thoughts and feelings (FEEL). I've applied Steps 1 – 3 to begin my transformation.

Now, use your *Life Timeline Journal* to write down a reflection of what thoughts/feelings have come up for you while reading thus far.

Exercise: Step 1 – TAG IT!

Do you have a recurring behavior pattern or theme that's been showing up for you? Tag it. Identify on your *Life Timeline* the day you realized this unconscious trait. Typically, this would take place at the moment you become aware, "This is an issue for me." What are some issues that you may need to tag? Relationship issues? Unhealthy behavior patterns? Negative thoughts? Addictions? Forms of escape? What are you trying to escape from?

Exercise: Step 2 – REMEMBER IT!

Next, identify when you inherited that download or when that way of thinking began. This is the neuro-circuitry of wiring in your brain that's been a program running on autopilot. Go back and remember the first instance of that tagged issue, behavior, or thought. Maybe it was demonstrated to you by a parent or caretaker? Did you experience trauma or pain that could be related to this perspective? As you learned in Chapter 2, the brain of a child from birth to seven years old is extremely permeable. Challenge yourself to recall back as far as you can to assess when that way of thinking took root in your subconscious mind. Write down the memory of the experience and indicate the age in which this took place on your *Life Timeline*. If you notice that this memory—or an instance that matches the theme—shows up multiple times, plot each instance on the *Life Timeline* at the age of inception. Remember, the story you tell yourself is the movie you produce. Oftentimes, we repeat stories and unconscious behavior patterns that turn into our reality.

Exercise: Step 3 – FEEL IT!

(Please note: If you have suffered a traumatic experience, it's recommended you get support from a professional to guide you through this system).

After you have recalled all the memories from your past associated with this topic, reflect on the way you felt (at that time). Feel the emotions like you felt them back then. This step is not about how you feel today, it's intended to get you to feel the emotions from that past event now. Feel the emotions in order to uproot them from your energy body. Explore where there may be unprocessed pain, shame, or guilt. Allow yourself to feel it. Write down the age at which you experienced these emotions. Be descriptive during your journaling process. Take as much time and space as you need to really unpack these memories and emotions.

For example, I explained the unconscious feelings of resentment towards my mother, along with the way I react to her at certain times. I've tagged this unconscious behavior pattern. Now, I'm going to recall why I may have this feeling. I realize it began around eight years old. I remember that feeling of being stuck amid my parents' fighting, assuming the projections of anger and resentment. I can Tag it on my *Life Timeline*—at the age I made this realization.

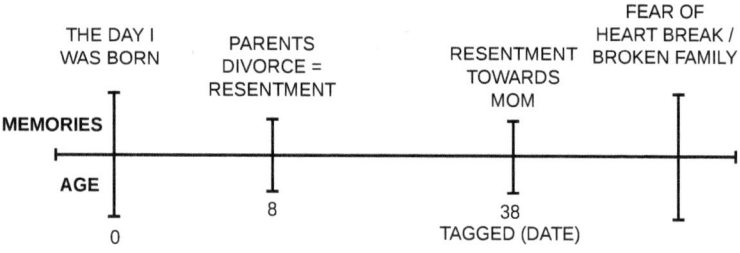

What are my issues today (at thirty-eight)?

~ Unconscious feelings of resentment toward my mother.
~ Fear of going through a divorce, which is why I've never been married.
~ Feeling like a misfit with a broken family. Alone. No father.
~ No sense of home stability. I've moved more times than I can count.

What are my triggers?

~ I feel like Mom projects her unhappiness onto me and expects me to help fill her voids (I'm sure this is an unconscious behavior pattern as well and I probably do the same to her). A mirrored reflection perhaps?
~ Because of my dismay for judgment, I notice that Mom judges and criticizes others. She is always talking about someone else and what they have going on in their life. To me, it's none of my business. Who are we to judge?

- I am overly critical of myself and continuously reflect on how I can improve. Maybe Mom's behavior has unconsciously compelled me to self-reflect deeper than I probably should?
- I yearn for someone to love and support me and my son unconditionally. Someone I can rely on without worrying of the "what-ifs!"
- I cut people out of my life quickly if I get the sense they could hurt me.
- I need to have control over situations, otherwise I feel powerless.
- I do or say things unconsciously that remind me of my mother's behavior and that makes me upset.

This step helps you get conscious of your struggles and curious about their root cause. Identify where experiences from your past may be having a negative impact on your results today.

In my childhood, for example, the broken family viewpoint continued to manifest. My Dad found a relationship with a woman who didn't like kids, so our bond dwindled to nothing. Mom was never home, so I spent all my time with Kim and her husband, Jim. For me, this was cool, because they taught me to drive a stick-shift Geo Tracker at ten years old. I spent the next three years going back and forth from Mom's house for school during the week to Kim and Jim's house on the weekends, hanging out with eighteen to twenty-one-year-olds. We'd get drunk, ride four-wheelers, and party. I was growing up fast; watching porn, doing shots and beer bongs, and staying up late. By thirteen, I did everything except have sex.

Please take time now to complete the exercises associated with Steps 1 – 3 in your *Life Timeline Journal*.

Your Perspective

It wasn't all bad. The next step is to flip your perspective. Kim and Jim taught me a great deal about finance, communication, leadership, and what it looks like to make a marriage work. They had an enormous influence on my *Life Timeline*. They loved me and cared for me when my parents didn't seem to. They were my rock and provided a stable foundation for me as a preteen. They tried to get me to move in with them and change schools, but I chose not to. My sister struggled with anxiety, depression, and OCD. Her obsessions became a diligent persuasion attempt to get others to conform to her beliefs. I am far from a conformist. It didn't feel right inside of me when they talked about people, or judged and criticized others, even their friends. They thought they were better than everyone else—they called some people "trash." Their point of view always seemed to have a negative lens. When someone is depressed, it's hard for them to see through a positive lens. Maybe it made her feel better to belittle others? I played along, laughed with them, but didn't agree with those actions intuitively. It was time for me to move on and figure out who I was with a tribe of kids my own age.

We don't realize how critical childhood experiences can be in shaping our outlook for the future and our personalities. I learned to break rules, surpass my own limitations, criticize others, consume alcohol, and get comfortable being uncomfortable. My program was developing as I transitioned into a teenager. Everything I learned and experienced from six to thirteen was stored in my subconscious program—available at any time to reference during my development. It set the stage for the rest of my *Life Timeline*.

Before we move on, I invite you to notice how this story makes you feel. Can you relate to this little girl; her feeling of loneliness, the need for stability, structure, love, or family? Do you have memories from your childhood that still affect your lifetime today? Lean in and get curious as you notice situations that may have developed your character as a result. Identify triggers from your past that may have formed habits or tendencies you carry out on autopilot, or have been replaying for a good part of your life. Now, you can notice them for what they are: subconscious programs. It's our ability to realize this that enables us to change. This is when it's important to understand and apply the *7-Step Life Timeline System of Transformation*.

This process and the steps that follow require support and repeated, focused attention. You can't overcome a twenty-year unconscious program overnight. As noted above, it takes at least ninety days to reprogram a new way of thinking. To get the best results, it's recommended that you have a coach or accountability partner to help support you along this journey. Infinite SOULutions is here to help **and support you**!

Chapter 5
The Teenage Screen

Searching for Love

"Not until we are lost do we begin to understand ourselves." [22]
—Henry David Thoreau

What you see on the surface will never reveal the depth of someone else's reality. As we progress through our *Life Timeline*, we accumulate levels of conditioning that shape our perception of the current moment. I focused my attention on finding a crew to fit into.

It was 1993. We elected Bill Clinton President and *Beverly Hills 90210* was the popular TV show. I was thirteen and about to go through one hell of a transition—my life would never be the same. As I entered seventh grade, I felt like an outsider. I was more mature than most kids my age. I felt lost, alone, and just wanted to fit in. It was time to find my identity. Most teens struggle to find their identity during this critical stage, and I started off with a foggy screen. Seventh grade is when everything shifted in my life. I wish I could go back in time, give this girl coping strategies, give her a hug, tell her I love her, and share the wisdom I know now. I wish she'd had someone to talk to who could have given her the guidance she needed. I wonder now, is that part of my life path? Did I go through these struggles to show other girls there is hope for a bright future, that you don't have to feel alone? Too many teenagers deal with feelings of inadequacy and endure experiences worse than mine without support or guidance.

It seems like high school is all about popularity. I wanted to be part of the popular crowd. In the summer before seventh grade, I became friends with a so-called "popular girl" and hung out with her group of friends. My two new best friends liked black boys. That was the trend going into my high school—white girls were hanging out with black boys who played football and basketball. We went to their games to see them play, and we hung out after school, even if that meant lying to our parents.

I was not raised to like black people. My dad was prejudiced and passed that conditioning down to my sister and me. They projected their racism onto me. Dad would say, "They are greasy, dirty, and overall, bad people." Because of that screen, I did not agree with the decisions my friends were making, but I wanted to fit in, so I went along. In the early nineties, interracial dating was not accepted—or at least it wasn't in my hometown in Pennsylvania. This was an interesting time in history, with the rise of RAP music and popularity across television media. Black Entertainment Television (BET) was becoming mainstream. This was all new to me, and I never liked to judge people, so I gave the guys a chance. I got to know them without judging them and realized that so-called "black people" did not differ from me. I saw them for their true selves, not for the color of their skin. They weren't dirty or bad. Then I met *him*—Trey. He was the high school football star. Everybody knew Trey. He had a girlfriend who was, of course, the high school girls' basketball star. Our group of friends started hanging around together and flirting like teenagers do. Trey flirted with me, but I wasn't interested—he had a girlfriend. Trey's best friend began dating my friend, and they all came to my house after school. There was rarely any parental supervision. We four girls (they called us "THE CREW") were looking for our identities (and I was looking for a way to fit in). Trey and I started messing around—and the spark ignited. A fourteen-year-old girl was looking for love, attention, and a sense of family, and she found it! This love flipped my life upside down and inside out for the next nine years. I learned more life lessons from the age of fourteen to twenty-three than I care to share.

My subconscious program was still in the download phase. The teenage screen, that lens that teens view life through, can be a complicated perspective to understand. It's not an easy time, as they try to figure out their way forward, fitting into cultural and societal norms at school, at home, and within social groups. There is so much competition, comparison, bullying, and judgment. The content in social media, music, and movies complicates the situation further. Our society gives more attention to the egoic mindset than to the spiritual side of nature. *A Course in Miracles* says, "Your mind can be possessed by illusions, but spirit is eternally free."[23] Ego is a construct of your mind. It's connected to the matrix—to the illusions of expectations, rules, and faulty programs. Illusions create a false sense of reality in the minds of many, which manifest later into belief systems that are passed down by families and cultures to younger generations. It's all a simulation of thought, and through observation/participation, you give it more energy. Energy to fuel the separation between people. Mean girls team up and leave you out. You feel isolated and alone. They make fun of you and talk about you behind your back. What are you to do? Your mind runs through so many scenarios, none of which makes you feel any better about the situation. Your heart hurts because your "so-called" friends are bashing your character.

Teenagers are trying to find their true self and independence while their bodies, powered by raging hormones, are changing. They want to be free to choose their path, but their parents, the school system, and their friends hold them to certain expectations. These opposing sides of the screen can cause continuous conflict. Parents have their own conditioning and want to shield their children from harm or from making the same mistakes they did, but teenagers don't see it that way. They can't fathom their parents' point of view, because they haven't yet experienced the situation. How can you learn something without experiencing it firsthand? Your parent says, "Don't play with fire or you will get burned." What do you do? Play with the fire until you get burned. The pain you feel will be stored in your subconscious memory bank to alert you of this possible sensation instantaneously the next time you are near fire. Mom tried to tell me that I would be judged and ridiculed for dating a black boy. I hadn't yet experienced this, nor did I care, because my love for Trey was stronger than my fear of being judged by others.

My teenage screen turned into a rebellion against the world of bullshit rules and racial injustice. I didn't agree with the expectations held over me by my family or community. When I was fourteen, on weekends my mother went to her boyfriend's place, leaving me the house to myself. My house became the Party Capital of Shenango Valley. I had the freedom to do whatever I wanted. Every weekend, my friends and I planned a house party. Teenagers did keg stands, smoked weed, and played Spades until the early hours of the morning. It was more like a college sorority house than a teenager's home. Come on over to Carrie's house! Kids would have sex in my mother's bed, in my bed, or on the couch. The radio was blasting. There were kids running in and out of the house. The neighbors called the cops often. We were "troubled" teens—at least that's what they called us. Some of my closest friends were not allowed at my house. They snuck over to hang out, anyway. We did a lot of lying to our parents. "The Crew and the Fella's" is what they called our clicks. Four white girls (best friends) who were dating four black boys.

I was Trey's creep for one year until it finally came out and he and his girlfriend broke up. When my family found out about him, they lost respect for me. My father, Kim, brother-in-law, aunts, uncles, cousins—the whole family—judged me for dating a black boy. My father disowned me. My sister and brother-in-law followed suit. What did I do? I rebelled. I shut them all out. I only wanted to be with Trey. My love for him consumed me, and nothing else mattered. I spent the next ten years on a ridiculous, unexplainable emotional roller coaster. Talk about judgment and criticism. Multiply it by five-hundred times when you are dealing with a white girl dating a black guy.

I was raised Catholic and went to church, but what they taught me didn't jibe with what fellow parishioners were saying about black people—and what they said about me! I had to choose—be (what they called) a "nigger-lover" or be (what I called) a racist. What kind of choice is that? I chose what my heart felt was right. I chose love, and they put me into a box. A box of judgment. There was no shiny red bow—it was a dark drape of shame. I was separated, scorned, and outcast. They rinsed me with not-so-holy water. The tears I cried rinsed my faith away.

I was living in the shadow of betrayal, shame, and criticism. My family and I were fighting. I ran away. I drank alcohol. I did drugs. I had sex. I skipped school. I got into fights. Their judgment and criticism made me feel resentful and sick to my stomach. As I write these words, it still does. It's disgusting how that belief system can tear families apart. That is what it did to my already-broken family. It broke me more.

Every day felt like a battle. Fights at home and in school, fist fights in the streets, and nasty messages communicated through pagers and payphones. I got tired of fighting and lying. I just wanted to be with Trey. I prayed my family would see past his skin color. One day after school, my mother and I got into a fist fight. I ran away from her, out of the house, with no shoes on, just my socks. Crying, hurt, and feeling unloved, I walked across town to my grandmother's house. As soon as I got there, my mother pulled into the driveway. I took off running through the back yard. Where was I going to go? We didn't have cell phones. I spent the next four hours walking to the other side of town, in my socks, to my best friend Luana's house. It was now dark and raining. I was cold, wet, and lost in a world of inexplicable chaos. It was 11:00 p.m. on a school night. Before climbing the huge hill Luana lived at the top of, I climbed inside the covered slide at the playground at the bottom of her street and rested for a bit. Finally, I made my way up the hill and threw rocks at her window. Luana was astonished to find me in the dark, needing a place to stay. I couldn't stay with her, but she walked me up the street to her cousin's house. I stayed with Luana's cousin for the next two days and didn't go to school. We hung out, smoked weed, and Trey came over to see me.

 I cared about my grades and didn't want to miss any more school, so I got a ride to school the next day. Not such a great idea when you are a full-fledged runaway. By lunchtime, word had gotten out that I was at school. The Sharon police showed up at lunchtime, handcuffed me in front of everyone, walked me out the back door, put me in the back of the cop car, and transported me to the third-floor psychiatric ward in the hospital. I spent three agonizing days with a bunch of mentally unstable patients. The staff came into my room a few times each night with flashlights to make sure I was still there and breathing. The counselors met with me and discovered that I wasn't unstable—I was just a teenager in love with someone her family didn't approve of.

 Racism and separation are taught, and without compliance, you can be punished. I resented and hated my mother with everything in me. I spent those three days resonating hatred. I'd run away from home because she told me I was going to ruin my life; that people would always judge me; that it was a disgrace; that I was breaking her heart. Did she think locking me up in a psychiatric ward would change my behavior? I didn't care what other people thought about me. Maybe she was concerned about how they viewed her because of my choices? Why do we allow the perceptions of others to define our decisions and ultimately our happiness? Why do we force our children into a pool of passed-down beliefs, judgments, and separation? I didn't get it. If I don't agree with something, I will not conform; I will walk the other way. I didn't agree with racism. I didn't agree with my family's judgment. I was a rebel with a lost cause.

No one recognized the pain I was going through. The judgment and disgust I felt from my sister was like a dagger in my heart. She had always been my sense of stability up until now. My father's disownment reemphasized the emptiness in my heart and my yearning for love from a man. He had already checked out of his fatherly duties, so this was a good excuse to seal up the coffin and leave his past behind. It felt like I was watching my favorite puppy die before my eyes. It made little sense to me. How could someone who said they loved me leave me to suffer in despair, all because of the color of someone's skin? It ripped the innocence of my heart out of my body and my soul. What did I do wrong? How could they abandon me, disown me, stop loving me? My pain turned into strength, but negatively.

Teenage years are hard enough without having to justify why your family has turned their backs on you. As a young girl, I learned to treat everyone the same and to show kindness and compassion. Now, nothing was making sense. So, I decided to NOT CARE! That was the best defense mechanism I could find. I would say over and over again to myself, *"I don't care. I don't care. I don't care."* If you don't care, you can't get hurt.

Watch what walls you build, because they can be difficult to break down or overcome later in life. I built many walls during my teenage years. By the time I entered my twenties, I had a fortress as big as the one in Super Mario Brothers where you fight Bowser to save the princess… there was even a lava pit carved along the outside layer of my fortress. No one could hurt me again! Come on and try, I dare you! I had to develop tough skin to make it through. I was a lost fifteen-year-old who got sucked into a typhoon of anger, jealousy, and ridicule (and tornadoes of other bad stuff). I found love in Trey—but did he love me?

What is love when you are a teenager? Did anyone teach us what love was? Or did we see it from a screen of our childhood upbringing? I didn't witness a loving marriage. My parents fought. That's all I remember. What is love as an adult? I know now that true love is not lust or yearning for someone to complete you. You need to be complete in your own body before letting someone else in to share that sacred gift. I wasn't complete. While I loved Trey more than anything on earth, my entire family (other than my mother) disowned me and called me every bad name under the sun. Even worse, while I was being judged for being with him; Trey cheated on me.

A Broken Heart

I lay on the cement walkway at Sharon High School, crying hysterically. I banged the back of my head on the pavement. "How could this happen?" My friends tried to pull me up off the ground, but my legs had given out. I couldn't move. I had just hung up the payphone—Trey had told me his ex-girlfriend was pregnant. It felt like he'd ripped out my heart. I didn't want to be anymore… be anything or be anywhere. I wanted to die. Nothing mattered. Looking back on it now, there were too many times during our nine-year relationship that I'd wanted to die.

I couldn't understand Trey's choices—and I didn't want to believe the truth. I wanted to follow my heart. But what happens when your heart leads you into a slaughterhouse? I had sacrificed so much for him. My intuition whispered, "Maybe that's a sign, Carrie? Chalk it up and move on. Let him go, move on. Stop wasting your time and tears!" No, that would have been too easy. That would have saved me so much heartache, tears, and time. No, I stood by him, supported him, cherished him, and believed in him. I could not live without him. I didn't want to.

How do you get through to a teenager in love? How do you connect with her pain and give her the guidance she needs without pushing her farther off the edge? She was on the edge of breaking. Her boyfriend was going to have a baby with someone else. Where did she fit into the picture now? She had no sense of family and no one loved her. She knew what was best but chose not to listen to her intuition. Who knew what was best for her, anyway?

Her parents?

Teachers?

Friends?

Her cheating boyfriend or his friends?

His ex, who is about to have his baby?

Her INTUITION?

Trey lied, cheated, apologized, made promises, and broke my heart for years—like a never-ending fractal. It became a pattern. I fought other girls for him. I fought my family for him. I filled the shoes of an outcast. I remember the looks my friends' parents and even teachers gave me, like I was an idiot. I felt like an idiot. I played his lies and stories over and over in my head while sitting outside his house in my mom's red Pontiac Sunfire. The shackles of shame, resentment, and disgust made the brick building at the bottom of his street seem like a simple solution. I envisioned throwing the car into drive and flooring the gas pedal for six seconds to reach max speed so I could crash into that brick building and die. I was sixteen.

Why did I allow this pattern to continue? I was a lonely, lost teenager seeking love in all the wrong places. Maybe it was because I didn't love myself? Great question, right? I'm sure many young women can relate. As an outsider looking in, the answer seems so simple. Yet, the outsider isn't viewing the situation from behind your screen. It's easy for us to judge another person, be it your friends or family members. It's easy to say, "You should leave him" when you don't have to feel the loneliness and pain of love lost. A teenager, head over heels in love, is a complex screen to get through, especially when they don't have a supportive foundation. I was hard-headed, resilient, and rebellious. Maybe it's my German side, but as a kid, I had to learn everything the hard way.

With bitter resentment, I learned how to co-parent someone else's child. How to fight other girls over a boy who cheated on me, turning it into a game or competition. How to live without a supportive family. How to dance in the rain when the tears poured down my face from the pain of betrayal. How to build walls. How to rebel further every time he cheated and lied. How to discard his apologies and promises. How to stop crying and stop caring. How to shut off my feelings to avoid being hurt anymore. How to run, escape the drama, and guard my heart.

I was the catalyst for change, at first, when Trey cheated on his girlfriend with me. I knew what I was doing. Maybe that is karma? One year later, I became his girlfriend, and he cheated on me with his ex-girlfriend. After that, his pattern repeated with other girls. They became the catalyst for change and interrupted our relationship. Reading this, you're probably thinking, "What relationship?" How can you stay with someone who continues to lie and cheat? *They* interfered with our relationship, destroying the trust, and breaking our connection? Wait! Who destroyed it? Who was responsible? Who made these decisions? Trey did. He was conscious of his intentions. It wasn't a mistake. His consciousness led him into each scenario, as did mine.

Remember that intuitive whisper, belly butterfly, or sick feeling? It's the silent alert from Source trying to show you that you are on the wrong path. I chose the path I was on, but I was also reaping the karma that came with it. I fought the other girls he slept with. Fist fights were arranged in parking lots; spectators watched as two white girls fought over this black boy who watched on the sidelines with his friends. That is not love. I would classify this as an egoic way to serve evil intentions. I would have moved mountains for him. I would have given up my life for him. That's a lot of time and energy spent in conflict.

Life is not meant to be lived in conflict. Our bodies are not meant to endure continuous stress and disharmony. In a world of things unseen, energy forces take a toll on our beings, on our way of thinking, feeling, and acting. This state of being turns into your subconscious program as you progress through your *Life Timeline*. Certain experiences can create strong negative energy that will follow you for years. I didn't know how to process the overwhelming emotions I felt, so they turned into dark, bottled-up energy. I shoved it deep down, locked up my heart, and focused on escaping the pain with drugs and alcohol.

> "Whatever we plant in our subconscious mind and nourish with repetition and emotion will one day become a reality." [24]
> —Earl Nightingale

Which side of the screen do you see this story through?

Exercise: Reflect upon Your Teenage Screen

Reflect on These Questions in Your *Life Timeline Journal*. Apply Steps 1 – 3 if you notice remnants of a program that took root during your adolescence.

~ Have you dealt with a similar situation? Heartbreak or Lost Love?
~ When reading this chapter, would you consider yourself as the empathetic observer, critical judger, or personal player? Why?
~ How does your perspective as a teenager differ from your perspective today? Why do you think that is?
~ If you are a teenager, how do you think your perspective may shift later in life?
~ What type of programming did you download from **your teen years**?

Chapter 6
Filling the Void

Unfulfilled Expectations

> *"I know that I will never find my father in any other man who comes into my life because it is a void in my life that can only be filled by him."* [25]
> —Halle Berry

As human beings having a spiritual experience, we don't realize we go through these seasons of life for a reason... maybe to see our reflection. It's all a hologram of our own wants and needs. We seek to be fulfilled from the outside in. That reflection is backwards. You can't find what you need on the outside. It has to come from within. Just look in the mirror and you will see. The little girl separated from her father, filled with resentment of her mother, and yearning for love and stability. She filled the void by giving unconditional love away, expecting to receive the same in return. Instead, the void grew.

Through each experience, I learned that you cannot change someone, no matter how hard you try. If they lie and cheat, that is their pattern. You cannot change it. I tried to help Trey improve his life for several years. I left for college, only to move back a year later to be with him. I transferred to a college he was attending to help him improve his grades so he could play football. He was a football star and had letters to get into any college he wanted, but he didn't have the grades. I was committed to being his forever. Even with all the pain and heartbreak, I continued to expect a different outcome. I wanted to have a family with him. That is, until the day he confessed he had gotten another woman pregnant—baby number two on my watch. That was it. I *FINALLY* made it official; we were done. I packed up the U-Haul and pulled away from that life for good. My family had wanted peace and happiness for me, and now

I would have the opportunity to find that. I was completing a chapter of my life that haunted me for a decade or more.

Now, as I write this book, reflecting on my *Life Timeline*, I realize I have carried blame, shame, and resentment in my energy body and projected it onto my mother, father, and sister subconsciously for over twenty years. I am activating the *Life Timeline System of Transformation* as I write this book. I remember and resonate with those thoughts and feelings. What happened to that little girl? During her adolescence, she got lost in the river of racism, constant conflict, lies, criticism, betrayal, and stereotypes from others' egoic mindsets. She left her soul behind a screen of shame shaded by their judgment. Sick of being weak and defeated, she learned to project strength and determination.

Exercise: Projecting Unfulfilled Expectations?

Reflect on these questions in your *Life Timeline Journal*.

- Did you experience having any unfulfilled expectations during your adolescence?
    - List them in detail.
    - Then observe where you may feel that same sense of being unfulfilled in your life today.
- Could you be projecting unsettled negative emotions or unfulfilled expectations into your current environment or relationships? If so, how, and why? What is the source of this projection?
- Apply Steps 1 – 3 to each scenario that applies. You should also be mapping these memories on your *Life Timeline* in order to uncover patterns that you may not be aware exist.

The Escape

Why didn't I wise up and take control of my life sooner? I felt like a victim in a hurricane of hate, depression, and solidarity. I tried to take my life a few times. I cried myself to sleep and wished that death would take me. Death would be easier. I was broken. Trey had broken me, taken my virginity, stolen my trust. My heart was ripped out by racism and run over by lies. While in a relationship with me, he'd had two children with two different women. That is not love.

I had allowed my outside environment to steal my power and dictate my happiness for too long. I would never allow myself to feel this type of pain again. My program was complete. My Carebear persona grew into a tough, NO-CARE Bear. I didn't give a shit about anything anymore. I was numb, so I sealed up my heart and shut out my soul. I turned into a master mason and crafted bricks around my heart. The mortar between the bricks hardened into the cold cracks that became my way of being. It was like sleeping alone in a dark dungeon on a cold, wet floor.

Alcohol helped dull the pain. I smoked weed to forget the past. I tried cocaine to have fun and party hard. Different men helped me feel like I was filling a void. When my family tried to talk to me or see me, I pushed them farther and farther away. What could they offer me now?

I was twenty-three years old and no longer a little girl looking for love. I was a grown woman filled with pain—it never left me. I was angry, isolated, fearless, and downright sick of it all. "Fuck them all, watch them fall," were the words I used to say. The program was running on autopilot. I practiced being strong, not caring, walking away from situations I couldn't control—just being me. I didn't think I had anything to live for. I didn't have a child, no genuine sense of family, no one to love who loved me. I had friends, and they became my family. My friends and I did one thing great, we partied. We did drugs. I sold drugs and bounced around from town to town, making money. My friends came up to me in bars, acting like puppies begging for "Scooby Snacks." I'd break a Vicodin in half, pop one half into their mouth and the other into mine. I bought everyone shots with the money I was raking in from selling pills and cocaine. A bunch of misfits, we had fun—we escaped our pain, lost love, and loneliness. The escape turned into nothing…

Nothing frightened me.
Nothing hurt me.
Nothing mattered.
Nothing felt good.

Only the escape; the NOT caring. I focused on freeing myself from feeling. I was numb like ice and didn't care. I partied like there was no tomorrow! Some nights, I didn't even sleep. But I always completed my college work and showed up to ace the test. This was important to me and my self-worth as a senior studying Business Management at Youngstown State University. I can recall a time when my friends and I were partying, and I did lines of cocaine until 7:00 a.m. when I had class at 9:00 a.m. I couldn't miss my Finance class and had a final in the class that followed, so I decided to just go. On my way to class, I stopped to get a twelve-pack of Bud Light so I would have something to drink afterwards and celebrate my achievement. I can't believe I made it through Finance class that day. Geeked out of my mind, I showed up in class, reeking of beer and cigarettes. As soon as the professor shut the door, I felt like I was going to puke. This wasn't such a good idea! My ambition at the time was greater than my darkness. That day, the professor called on me. He never called on me! He knew! I knew! My screen was revealed.

As soon as class let out, I ran from the building and skipped the final in the class that followed. I called my friends and said, "Have two lines ready for me. I'll be back in twenty minutes." We got high, drank for another six hours, then passed out for the rest of the day. "C-Money" (that's what my friends used to call me) was rolling in cash, having fun, and getting paid to party. My phone was blowing up like a baller. I'd party until 5:00 a.m., sleep most of the next day, wake up, drink, make another deal ... rinse and repeat. Day after day, I dulled the disgust deep in my heart with whatever form of escape I could find. No one cared about me—in fact, I didn't care about myself.

Can you see the mirror? My belief that no one cared about me caused me to act without regard for myself or others. The paradox of perception. A web of observer angles and pieces of the mirror projecting reflection and pain. The escape of getting high... forgetting about the past... running away from unresolved problems. I wanted to escape life. That's what drugs and alcohol do. They allow you to escape the bonds of your mind, masking your reality until they turn into a habit. You gain another vice with long-term effects for your *Life Timeline*. It's deceptive, the ego, it reels you into a high that feels like a brilliant solution—until you deal with the low the next day. The day after doing cocaine, I felt like death walking. What did it matter? My spirit was numb, anyway. I didn't care about much; I was having fun, but not in a positive way. It was not a good path. I had lost my will. That was my screen. Fuck them all, watch them fall. I was not a bad person. I still had a heart. It was just on ice.

"To different minds, the same world is a hell and a heaven." [26]
—Ralph Waldo Emerson

The Lonely Road

I've been walking a long, gravel road that turned into
a steep and challenging climb.
The days are longer than the nights.
The pain runs deep. It's tucked away, back in the shadows,
behind a wall of rock.
We are all hiding behind that rock, drenched with shame.
We exist in the shadows of loneliness—not reaching out—not
getting connected—fighting the battle alone—wallowing in our
regret, silencing our sadness, and hiding our fear...
The days drift by.
The holidays come and go.
Here we are—alone, wanting a different outcome—still
getting the same results.
You tried, once or twice, to step out—to change—
to change your story.
It was difficult and scary.
The unfamiliar territory made you feel even more alone,
so you reverted quicker than you could talk yourself
into reaching for more.
It's more comfortable here in my solidarity.
So, I repeat the same story, stumbling over the gravel rocks
along the way.

Misfit in Disguise

Without a sturdy foundation (family and home), sense of self-worth, or feeling of love, I sought what I needed from other people or in different forms of escape. I became conditioned to fit in with misfits. I felt like a misfit and perceived that other people judge me as a misfit. Did they? Behind my screen, that's what I thought and felt. I've carried that with me into adulthood.

Broken family = misfit
Interracial relationship = misfit
Drug and alcohol abuse = misfit
Single mother = misfit

This holographic image of myself continues to play on my screen because I am different. That perception has reflected in my *Life Timeline* results. This is where our self-reflection process can get tricky, but it's necessary to see through the veil of the reality you co-create. I broke the rules, challenged the status quo, and avoided feeling. Far from any type of God, rebelling down a lonely, dark road, I hit rock bottom on Christmas Day, 2005.

On Christmas Eve, I partied with friends at different house parties, then ended up at the bar. The bartender kicked me out when I fell off my barstool, so we took the party to my friend Terry's house. The next day, I woke up on Terry's couch with an agonizing hangover. I looked and felt like death. So, I stayed on the couch in the dark on Christmas Day, talking to no one but a friend lying on the couch across from me. We didn't have family gatherings to attend, or Christmas presents to worry about. Depressed and alone, I thought, "What a way to spend Christmas Day!"

Later that evening, I went out to re-up (buy more cocaine to sell) and got robbed! I picked up a drug dealer (I had a few options), drove to the projects, and handed him $600 to buy an ounce for me. He took my money, walked into the projects, and never came back. I sat in my car, waiting and waiting—only to realize he wasn't coming back. I broke down crying. Broken. Alone. Separate from the whole on Christmas. They say, "When it rains, it pours." I was drenched in desperation. Maybe this was my karma? So many people are stuck in an isolated state. If this resonates with you, I pray that light will shine your way through my words. There is hope and a better path. Thank God, I found it the following year. Although I didn't find it, **God planted the seed in me.**

Chapter 7
A Catalyst for Change

Egoic Illusions

> *"It's the beauty within us that makes it possible for us to recognize the beauty around us. The question is not what you look at but what you see."* [27]
> —Henry David Thoreau

We have all lost our power at some point in this finite lifetime—we sacrifice it to the ego often. There's a voice in your head that says you're not good enough, smart enough, or loved. It ridicules your aspirations, points out your insecurities, and projects your pain onto others unconsciously. That sense of self keeps you feeling small, ugly, and defeated. It tells you your nose is too big, you need makeup to look pretty, or your arms are flabby. It paints pictures in your head of a false reality. It forces you to feel self-conscious and makes you think you need a man or woman to make you feel loved. You lose your power to the false perceptions it plants in your mind.

This way of thinking is reemphasized when we indulge in the illusion of perfection personified through social media, television, and advertisements. Our desire for *more* enhances our self-loathing, creating a culture of people plagued with jealousy and envy. Teenagers are stuck between a generational world view that's been shifting before our eyes: all the social norms, traditions, and standards we once relied on are changing. Nothing is certain anymore. We are sacrificing the health of our planet, animals, and people to the need and greed of the egoic mindset, and it's depleting our ability to survive. Overpopulation, overconsumption, deforestation, technological and industrial development, and pollution deplete our natural resources, leaving a gap that will destroy humanity. The ego has mastered the matrix, allowing its darkness to shadow the fact that we are killing our planet and disempowering people. We are mistreating one another, which influences the collective. The ego plays with our perceptions and negatively influences our state of being. This internal struggle causes stress and unhappiness, because the pull from our divine spirit is at odds with the egoic lens of our monkey mind. Millions of people suffer from this internal struggle daily. The soul-sucking illusion of fear has been slowly depleting our power for too long, allowing the pharmaceutical industry to prosper as mental illness reaches an all-time high. Suicide has become a teenage epidemic, while drug addiction is ruining our cities. You see the destruction on the news, hear hatred in music, and watch films filled with conflict and fear on Netflix. Our participation fuels the beast of corruption. Depression and anxiety are real—the depths of their darkness can destroy relationships and livelihoods.

Mental Health Crisis

The catalyst for change can be disruptive. Human beings don't like change. The uncertainty of events, people's reactions, and disorder can scare people into believing false information. The majority rules and the news feeds the fear. 2020 introduced a catalyst. Change was forced on every human being walking this planet. The outbreak of this virus could have been intentional or random. Either way, it delivered a drastic wake-up call to humanity. I will never argue with another person over whose beliefs are right—yours or mine—because it all depends upon your perspective or the screen you are currently viewing life through. You can't see mine and I can't see yours. But whatever our angle, something is forcing us to see life from a new perspective. We will never return to what we once perceived as "normal." Our population is facing global unrest from multiple perspectives behind a multiplicity of screens spanning seven billion people who don't know what to expect next. The only thing we know is that change is inevitable.

A drastic shift is taking place on this planet, spiritually, politically, culturally, and ultimately, energetically. Evolutionary changes are happening before our eyes, while the majority of people are disconnected and unconscious. We are asleep at the wheel of life, disconnected from Source. We are distracted by the illusions of our own screen, social conditioning, and governmental control. As a collective body of unconscious minds, guarded hearts, and lost souls, people are mindlessly walking through life, unaware of their power. The concept or belief that we are separate (individuals) from the whole (of humanity and nature) has been passed down to us. Cultural beliefs breed separation by race, region, religion, and income—distracting us from the truth that we are all connected. There is only one Source, and we are united through the power breathing us in human form. That power keeps our planet rotating and balanced. Our minds and bodies need balance. Without balance, disease will manifest. It's been slowly manifesting right before our eyes, yet we are too distracted to see. Americans live a wasteful and lavish lifestyle compared to the citizens of many other countries in the world. We take water, our food supply, and even electricity for granted. We cater to convenience and expect to have everything we need instantaneously or at our doorstep within two days. We consume and throw away more packaging waste than is imaginable. All this convenience comes at a cost—our planet's health. We are destroying the only home we have. We can't breathe without the oxygen our trees provide. We can't survive without water and food. Mexico City is running out of fresh water. Genetic engineering is negatively altering our food supply. The natural resources we rely on to survive are being depleted faster than ever. You and I may not see the impact of this, but our children and grandchildren will.

Therefore, I ask this important question, "What are we really living for?" To make another dollar or to make a difference in the world? To teach or torment? To live freely or under governmental control? To have a positive impact on others or to focus on our own selfishness? Is it your world or mine? How can we awaken humanity to see through the egoic illusions, take hold of their power to change the future, and make this world a better place to live and breathe? First, we need to get to the root of the problem. Your mind: it's either a garden for greatness or desolation. What you plant in your mind and believe will manifest over time. Mental health affects your physical health directly. The effects may not be immediate, but they will show up over time. When mental illness takes root in someone's life, without proper treatment, it can breed more misfortune. People search for ways to escape their discomfort. The escape may be found in a pill to ease the pain or a drug to get them high. From the microscopic to global perspective, we are oblivious to the long-term effects our choices can have. Maybe we don't want to see the truth? Conscious or not, our choices influence the collective. Collectively, we are impacted by these astonishing statistics:

~ Humanity is using nature 1.7 times faster than our planet's bio-capacity can regenerate. That's equivalent to using the resources of 1.7 Earths.[28]
~ According to the Centers for Disease Control and Prevention (CDC) WISQARS Leading Causes of Death Reports, in 2019: Suicide is the second leading cause of death among people aged ten to thirty-four, and the

fourth leading cause of among individuals between the ages of 35 and 44.[29]
~ One in five U.S. adults experiences mental illness each year. Among adults aged 18 or older in 2020, 21.0 percent (or 52.9 million people) had any mental illness (AMI) and 5.6 percent (or 14.2 million people) had serious mental illness (SMI) in the past year. [Of this group] 30.5 percent (or 16.1 million people) perceived an unmet need for mental health services in the past year.[30]
~ Among adolescents aged 12 to 17 in 2020, 17.0 percent (or 4.1 million people) had a past year major depressive episode.[31]
~ One out of every five students reported being bullied in 2019.[32]
~ Students who experience bullying are at increased risk of depression, anxiety, sleep difficulties, lower academic achievement, and dropping out of school.[33]
~ Depression...affects about 121 million people worldwide. World Health Organization (WHO) states that depression is the leading cause of disability.[34] Annual prevalence among U.S. adults, Anxiety Disorders: 19.1 percent (estimated forty-eight million people).[35]

Mental health determines your ability to live a healthy, productive, and happy lifestyle, yet our people deal with the effects of its wrath daily. Forty-eight million people suffer from persistent feelings of fear, worry, and uneasiness within everyday situations. Anxiety makes you feel like your heart is beating out of your chest. You can't breathe. You are overwhelmed and isolated in your own head. The "what-if's" of scenarios play out over and over within the analytical mind, causing your body to react as if it's in that situation of doom and gloom: "What if they laugh at me? What if I forget? What if I fail?" All that worry fuels your fight-or-flight nervous response, sending your body into a frenzy for no reason other than to satisfy your ego with its fearful antics.

One out of every five people is living in a state of stress. Bullying at school and online is a huge problem and has extreme consequences. Not only are these statistics shocking, but the fact that our Western culture is conditioned to prescribe and take medication instead of being taught how to deal with their emotional health and stressful situations is disgusting. Doctors write a prescription and move on to the next patient without identifying the root cause of a patient's suffering. They don't know what's going on at home, in school, or in a child's mind. They listen for the symptoms and offer a Band-Aid, because it's easier and less time-consuming that way. Insurance companies dictate the type of treatment we receive. These children grow into adults who need depression or anxiety medication, but that never solves the underlying problem. They are stuck in a fog until a catalyst for change is introduced—until the Universe delivers a wake-up call to get them to **see the light.**

Intuitively, you know that pill isn't solving your real problem. It's just masking the screen. Children turn into adults and parents who have unresolved trauma and experiences that need to be dealt with and released from their energy body. Otherwise, that energy is passed on and the ego wins by crippling your ability to function in social gatherings, at work, or within family activities. It's easier to hide out in the bathroom, escape into a bottle of vodka, or smoke a blunt in the garage than to partake in those dreadful activities. Your vice turns into your haven.

According to the American Psychiatric Association (APA), fifty percent of mental illness begins by age fourteen, and three-quarters begin by age twenty-four.[36] The APA says that "Mental illnesses are health conditions involving changes in emotion, thinking or behavior (or a combination of these). Mental illnesses are associated with distress and/or problems functioning in social, work or family activities."[37] That is a broad assessment, don't you think? In doing research on this topic, I found there are over 200 diagnosable mental illnesses. This illness affects many people's livelihoods, and it has a daunting ripple effect on their social relationships. We should talk about these issues that plague all of us instead of trying to hide them behind our screens. The more we hide our flaws and secretly judge others, the more we create suffering. You suffer *behind the screen*. That suffering affects every interaction you have and the reality you co-create.

My mental illness began at fourteen years old exactly. Recall that I was depressed because I felt my family hated me for the people I associated with while I was trying to fit into my high school social groups. Because of their judgment and criticism, I lost my power and became depressed. I slept a lot. I had terrible anxiety coupled with a bad attitude. I felt like no one understood my situation. Instead of getting the counseling support I needed to help deal with this state of being, my doctor prescribed Paxil, a depression medication. That made my head more foggy and heightened my emotional sensitivity. I went to school, came home, and cried myself to sleep. I hated my mother, father, sister, and everyone in my family. I hated my life. I didn't have anyone to talk to. I was alone, left to deal with the negative thoughts screaming in my head. A voice inside me told me dying would be easier. That pill the doctor prescribed me didn't change the fact that my family wasn't there for me or that my boyfriend cheated on me, nor did it prepare me for the fires I had to fight every day at school.

Depression medications are difficult to get off once you start taking them. We allow a billion-dollar global market to keep our children stuck in a foggy state of mind without giving them the tools they really need to find the light. Maybe our money would be better spent on different types of treatments? The problem is most insurance companies do not cover the non-traditional treatments that can be the most effective. I didn't learn about mindfulness or meditation until I was 32 years old at a conference in Los Angeles. I had no idea what chakras were or how powerful Kundalini Yoga can be. I stumbled upon this priceless information as an adult. Eastern cultures are conditioned to practice mindfulness, meditation, and yoga at a young age. The United States is very slow to catch on. It makes me wonder—are "they" trying to keep us stuck in this matrix of illusion—unaware of our true power? Whose agenda are we living to satisfy? The powerful corporations', governmental leaders', and elite people?

Fitting into the Box

As I stated before, our children need to learn about the power of our mind, body, and soul connection. They should learn about emotional intelligence and the proper way to deal with emotions. I've taught workshops about Emotional Intelligence for adults in the workplace, but why isn't this a focus in school? Teenagers are forced to ride an emotional roller coaster with no fundamental tools (other than medication to mask the uneasiness) to guide them through the highs and lows. Society has programmed us to believe we need what our governmental institutions and political leaders offer us: free education (in which the curriculum is controlled), health insurance to pay for medication, financial systems, and the 8:00 a.m. to 5:00 p.m. job. We must pay taxes. Follow the leader; try to fit in with the rest of society. Don't question authorities; they have our best interest in their hearts. Really?

What if you don't fit into their box? What if you can't sit still in school and you struggle with paying attention? School has been hell for my son since kindergarten because he has ADHD. As early as four, his daycare classified him as a "troubled child" and that label has followed him into every classroom since. As a single parent, I deal with the effects of this judgment and classification from teachers, principals, and childcare workers. Even though children with ADHD are intelligent and likely to succeed as inventors, entrepreneurs, or artists, they are demeaned and humiliated in grade school. If a child isn't taking medication to control their ADHD, they are likely failing. It's their hyperactivity and impulsiveness that gets them into trouble, so they become a target. These systems and classifications are sucking the souls out of our children behind our conscious awareness.

As a mother, I reflect over years of struggle and strife in dealing with the school system that expects every child to think and act alike. If you don't fit into this box, you are ostracized because you have a disorder. Why is this a disorder? My son is the most brilliant person I know. He has been inventing, designing, and building the most amazing contraptions for years. He can see other dimensions and has ways of thinking that most of us don't. That makes him special. Some of the most talented and successful people have ADHD: Adam Levine, Justin Timberlake, Will Smith, Michael Phelps, Carrie Underwood, Bill Gates, and Shaquille O'Neal, to name a few. True leaders don't follow their pack; they find a more creative route to take. They are not "normal." That's why they are classified differently. A bunch of misfits who can change the world. It's time to **flip the screen.**

Fractal Patterns

How well do you or your loved ones fit into society's cultural norms? What if your parents struggle with depression, anxiety, or their own disorder? What if they hide *behind the screen* and find their escape in drugs, alcohol, gambling, online shopping, or emotional eating? As a child, your subconscious program includes these experiences, so you become a new offspring of this fractal. What is a fractal? According to the Fractal Foundation, "A fractal is a never-ending pattern. Fractals are infinitely complex patterns that are self-similar across different scales. They are created by repeating a simple process over and over in an ongoing feedback loop."[38] Fractals can be found everywhere in nature and throughout the universe. Examples include clouds, snowflakes, river networks, flowers, tree leaves, and systems of blood vessels, to name a few. Fractal patterns can be found in music, your lungs, and artwork. Our Universe is breathing fractals. As mathematician Benoit Mandelbrot, the so-called "father of fractals" said, "*A fractal is a way of seeing infinity.*"[39]

Our lives are like a fractal pattern of repeating habits, suppressed emotions, and beliefs installed during our childhood upbringing. We become a product of our environment, and unless we are aware, we can repeat the same internal conflicts over and over throughout our adult lives. These patterns affect our relationships, health, academic/career progression, and emotional wellbeing—the pattern just continues like an ongoing feedback loop. You and I are part of the whole. We see the patterns continue to repeat through history, within cultures, through people, within communities, and through family traditions, until a catalyst for change is introduced, to shift energy or **interrupt the pattern.**

An Invisible Force

Could the catalyst be a virus? A virus that is...

~ Not bound by stereotypes.
~ Invisible to race, age, and gender.
~ Able to live in the bodies of the rich and poor, not divided by borders or religion.
~ Unseen. Unpredictable.
~ Forcing us to stop. To stop running on the hamster wheel. To stop walking mindlessly through life.

A *virus*. It brought our world to a screeching halt. The virus unites people across the planet but forces us to separate. Is it our catalyst for change? Will we see the truth or allow the ego to rule and divide us by our beliefs? Is the virus a force for good? Or a force of evil? Which lens will you view this from? Which side of the screen are you on?

Is the virus showing us what really matters?
~ Our truth: We are all connected. We are all the same. We need our planet. We cannot be blind any longer. We need each other.

Is it asking us to change?
~ To stop competing against one another. Stop fighting and feeding separation?
~ To start believing in something greater than the negative news stories?
~ To start collaborating and working together?
~ To spread love. Share light. Be the change we need to see in this world?

This is our time:
- ~ Time to awaken. Time to remove the blinders.
- ~ Stop running on the hamster wheel.
- ~ Time to change. Time to stop rushing.
- ~ Stop being so disconnected and distressed.
- ~ Time to start learning about Universal Laws that will transform lives.

A virus. It stopped production, travel, and socialization. Is it showing us how programmed we have become? Or could it be a ploy to control the growing population, thereby brainwashing us even further? Fooling us to focus more on our fear than faith. A catalyst uniting our world through fear, uncertainty, and worry... or dividing us by our decision whether to vaccinate, wear a mask, or conform to governmental control? Will it empower us as a species to stop and see what truly matters? Or will it keep us divided, arguing over **Whose Lives Matter?**

Exercise: The Looking Glass

British philosopher James Allen said in his book, *As a Man Thinketh*, "Mind is the master power that moulds and makes, and man is mind, and evermore he takes the tool of thought, and, shaping what he wills, brings forth a thousand joys, a thousand ills. He thinks in secret, and it comes to pass. Environment is but his looking-glass."[40]

What glass are you looking through during this reflection? Take time to explore the ideas that came up for you while reading this chapter. Write a reflection in your *Life Timeline Journal*.

- Have you dealt with any mental health issues? What about someone in your family or a close friend? How has this impacted your life?
- What type of belief systems did you inherit?
- What experiences did you survive that constructed your character? These are pieces of the puzzle that create your personality and personal reality. Are the pieces serving you now or strangling your ability to find peace and harmony within your *Life Timeline*?
- Do you love the person you are on either side of that screen?
- How are you contributing to the health of our planet?
- What could you do differently to make this world a better place?
- If you are a parent, how may you be passing some sort of programming onto your children (or vice versa)?

Chapter 8
Connect to your Power

The Great Discovery

"Unless man discovers that his consciousness is the cause of every expression of his life, he will continue seeking the cause of his confusion in the world of effects, and so shall die in his fruitless search." [41]
—Neville Goddard

Are you awake and ready to connect to your power, or will you stay stuck in the paradigm of injustice? Injustice in our systems that were built upon the concept of freedom. Injustice in our hearts that are meant to live and breathe in a state of harmony. Injustice among our species who collectively and ultimately yearn for one thing: *Love*. Therefore, where do we seek the justice necessary to put an end to the conflict we all experience? Time spent in conflict not only depletes your energy, but it is a waste of precious time. It creates an emptiness that must be filled or restored somehow. We look for something on the outside to fill our voids—someone else to love us, alcohol or drugs, shopping, eating, etc. You know the pattern, maybe even personally? The secret power is invisible. You can't see it, purchase it, or consume it. It's already inside you. You have the keys to access it anytime your will rises above the egoic lens. Go within. Find your inner peace. Balance. Practice forgiveness. Acceptance. Love. You can transform your life and impact the collective by raising your consciousness.

Truth, freedom, and peace stem from the soul. Our garden of greatness lies within the power of the Holy Spirit. It's our free will! "Our father, who art in heaven, hallowed be thy name, thy kingdom come, THY WILL BE DONE on Earth as it is in heaven." (Matthew 6:10) I learned and repeated the Lord's Prayer as a young girl, but never understood its power. It's all left to your own interpretation—everything reflects your belief or understanding. I believe this powerful prayer is telling us that you have God's Will within you. You are a part of the whole; through your will you can spread light and love on Earth. You co-create peace on Earth just as if you were in heaven. Heaven is a mindset. Consciousness is your Power—it's Universally connected through Source. Source is the "higher power" you believe in.

Your truth and power reside behind your screen. That is the great discovery. Through your act of being aware, present, and faithful, you can make a difference in the world. Choose faith over fear, and spirit over ego. Your consciousness can transform; rise from the darkness and reside in the light of love. BELIEVE in something greater than the seen, finite world. Believe in something greater than your financial hardships, pain, or heartbreak. Don't buy into political corruption or the agendas of others. You can overcome limiting beliefs and break through the walls of suffering. Reside in the knowing that your will *will* be done on Earth as it is in heaven. Believe (BE-LIVE) in Aliveness. Your will gives you the strength to overcome any injustice.

As a child, I believed in God (a higher power) and prayer. However, logically I couldn't make sense of the idea that there is a man called God in the sky. Despite being infinite, God is depicted from a finite viewpoint. We cannot quantify the spiritual realm or the creator of our universe. They are infinite and unlimited. I never truly understood the power of God, or the Infinitely Abundant Universe, until I was an adult and began searching for my purpose in this *Life Timeline*. A feeling that I have greater purpose and a higher calling to impact change on this planet forced me to seek spiritual information from various resources. I started to put the puzzle pieces together from a scientific and biblical perspective. When I viewed spirituality from a scientific perspective, it all started to make sense! That was the greatest discovery—and can be for you as well. To see outside the box, seek additional sources of information from different perspectives and let go of the programmed belief you were taught. The only thing a box can contain is our human body because our spirit can ascend. Our power is infinite and almighty—just like God. That's what Jesus tried to show us. He wasn't bound to the egoic forces of the mind. He understood the Universal Laws and acted upon them with sincere conviction. Discard the egoic point of view and let go of the need to control everything. When you "let go and let God," miracles happen.

Your mind, body, and soul... the power of three. The holy trinity. An electromagnetic force field you exude, this is your instrument to navigate the world of seen and unseen forces. We all have the power. We were born with it. We were not taught how to harness it and use it for good. They conditioned us to believe in our fear, limitations, and conditions. Luckily, you are on the right track. Through your screen, you may now see a glimpse of infinite possibility. Anytime, that is, you are ready to wake up and regain your consciousness.

CONNECT TO YOUR POWER

"No man can lift you to the level you desire. The power to ascend is within yourself; it is your consciousness…find the only and everlasting master within yourself." [42]
—Neville Goddard

Universal Consciousness

Human consciousness is rising. I believe people are waking up from the negative news and mass programming to realize they only feed its fire through their observation and participation. My goal is to help lead this spiritual revolution by sharing the information I've learned as an adult from several influential leaders of our time. Over the past ten years, I have read books like *Breaking the Habit of Being Yourself* by Dr. Joe Dispenza; *Girl, Wash Your Face* by Rachael Hollis; *A New Earth,* by Eckhart Tolle; *The Seat of the Soul* by Gary Zukav; and my favorite, *The Power of Intention,* by Dr. Wayne Dyer. The principles they teach empower me to think in new ways and act on my dreams. It has been a transformational experience and continues to be as I teach these life-changing principles to my family, friends, clients, etc. I hope people will seek this evolutionary wisdom, rise above their conditioning, and make this world a better place. Just look up these spiritual thought leaders on YouTube and watch a couple of episodes to learn more about our Universe and the power you hold: Mary Morrissey, Dr. Wayne Dyer, Les Brown, Marianne Williamson, Tony Robbins, Bob Proctor, Bruce Lipton, Gregg Braden, Dr. Theresa Bullard, and Michael Beckwith, all of whom teach about the power of your mind. They understand that you can co-create your reality by holding focused attention, coupled with a burning desire, grateful expectation (absent from fear, doubt, or worry) and faith. Your ability to manifest thought into form is accomplished through your consciousness. Your divine spirit, focused intention, willpower, and loving energy will shift the frequency of this planet. It seems simple, but it has proven tremendously difficult for most people to see this fruitful path. Now is the time to overcome our subconscious programs, connect to our power, and rise above the egoic lens that blinds us from our limitless potential. Break through those social conditions, cleanse your screen, and claim the life God intended you to live.

From a quantum perspective, the universe is divinely connected and infinitely intelligent. The great Albert Einstein proved by his equation, E=mc2, "that matter and energy are interchangeable. They are one and the same."[43] Our Universe is made up of energy. In fact, we are luminous light beings who give off energetic vibrational frequencies. Our emotions are simply energy in motion. All matter exists because of consciousness. Consciousness is defined as "the quality or state of being aware, especially of something within oneself... being conscious of an external object, state, or fact."[44] In other words, your consciousness is your awareness, and that invisible focus creates matter. Wherever you place your attention will manifest into your reality over the course of your *Life Timeline*, however long it may be. This is based upon the thoughts and feelings (invisible sources of energy) you emit into the ether of the Universe; according to your vibrational frequency at that moment. They emit either a positive or negative electromagnetic energy wave into the field of energy (the Quantum Field) which exists infinitely. All matter consists of atoms or subatomic particles that contain a nucleus (neutron and proton) with an electron that's always moving around the nucleus in wave form. When you view the electron, it collapses from a wave of probability into a particle of creation. This is known as the Observer Effect. Your observation is an act of creation or manifestation of physical reality. That's why you hear people say, "Don't give it your energy." They mean don't give something your attention unless you want to manifest more of this thing in your reality. Where your attention (your observation) goes → your energy (your power) flows. Now apply this equation to your life. When you watch the news, you are observing the details they provide—and most are funded by fear. That fear feeds your thoughts and can make you feel powerless, even stressed, or overwhelmed. When you pay attention to political scandals or engage in political posts within social platforms, you are giving that scandal or post more energy. When you focus on learning a new subject, you are giving your mental and emotional energy to the act of learning. When you focus on someone, you give them your energy—whether it be a thought or feeling. Have you ever had someone call you out of the blue when you were just thinking about them? You were in tune with one another at that very moment in time. Coincidence or divine connection?

    To put this into context, human beings feed off the energy of observation. That's why social media has exploded over the past ten years. When you like, share, subscribe, or host a watch party, from a subatomic perspective, you are giving that particle energy, or you are collapsing that electron of probability into a particle of creation. Social media is all about the likes, subscriptions, and shares. TV shows, movies, music, live streams, and social media stories continue to expand based upon your likes and views. The more you observe, the more you give energy to that which you observe. The richest people on the planet understand these universal laws. That's how they got to be rich. They are the ones creating and taking action. The people observing their actions essentially give them more power or energy to create. The enormous growth of social media is due to the influence of observation. Facebook led the way by adding the Like button. YouTube, Instagram, Twitter, and TikTok followed suit, allowing all these observations and interactions to affect our way of life, down to the smallest subatomic particle. People act differently based on being observed. Look at selfies, reality TV shows, watch parties, or consider FaceTime. Don't you act differently when talking via FaceTime or Zoom than you do just talking regularly with no camera on? People are affected by observation. It's the mere act of consciousness that transforms the invisible into the physical. This phenomenon is changing the way we live our lives... and it's not all fun and games. It's also used for unscrupulous purposes. Today, Google, Facebook, Amazon, and many others are using artificial intelligence to collect psychological data on every user, to construct algorithms, and to influence our purchasing decisions. They intentionally play ads to affect our behavior. *Behind the screen*, they monitor every interaction we have. We go from one extreme to the other, but it all starts with a thought or idea. Scientists have been searching since the sixth century BCE for the smallest particle in the Universe to figure out what makes up matter. The more they looked, the more particles were created. The mere act of observing (consciously) is an art of creation.

Flip the screen to see the scientific side of life. Don't go walking through life unaware that you are an energetic being made up of photons and electrons in the act of being observed or observing other electrons—that observation transforms energy on a repeating scale. "**Light energy** is defined as how nature moves energy at an extremely rapid rate, and it makes up about 99% of the body's atoms and cells, and signal all body parts to carry out their respective tasks."[45] You are a photon, in many ways a form of light energy, made up of trillions and trillions of photons interacting, vibrating, and learning from one another. They dance around with the electrons, entangling and exciting them. What happens when you get excited? You give off energy. Where did it come from? An excited electron maybe? I can get lost in the science behind spirituality.

Inventor Nikola Tesla, who laid the foundation for wireless technology, said, "If you want to find the secrets of the universe, think in terms of energy, frequency and vibration."[46] He also stated, "What one man calls God, another calls the laws of physics."[47] Instead of getting stuck in titles and names, step back and become objective about this approach and the world around you. What you pay attention to, or observe, will be affected depending upon your intention and frame of reference.

The scientific perspective has shifted from a classical Newtonian (linear) worldview to a Quantum (holistic) approach. It's been a controversial topic for scientists, mainly because it's difficult to measure and control an experiment when the mere act of observing or measuring alters the results. This phenomenon can be demonstrated by the infamous double-slit experiment first conducted by Thomas Young in 1804—it still baffles physicists today. "When scientists tracked the individual particles as they move through the slits, the monitored particles abandoned their wave-like state and showed up as two separate lines on the screen. It's as if they knew they were being watched."[48] The experiment revealed that subatomic particles can change quantum states exhibiting properties of a wave (an invisible force field) or properties of a particle (matter) depending upon the presence of an observer. To me, this gives us profound insight about the power of consciousness and its effect on reality as we see it.

The battle between good and evil, light and dark, has been going on since the beginning of time. Stories shared in biblical gospels were intended to get people to see this invisible realm and connect to their power. Separation has and always will exist, because there is a yin and yang. This philosophy shows how two opposing forces are actually interconnected. Masculine and feminine. Positive and negative. The Principle of Polarity, according to the Seven Hermetic principles, states that: "Everything is Dual; everything has poles; everything has its pair of opposites; like and unlike are the same; opposites are identical in nature, but different in degree;

extremes meet; all truths are but half-truths; all paradoxes may be reconciled."[49] Polarity exists in every aspect of evolution, including chemistry and biology, and it is even a part of our makeup on a cellular level. The balance of good (soul) and evil (ego) exists everywhere in our universe. A bible verse I wrote in permanent marker on my bedroom wall said, "Heaven is my throne, and the earth is my footstool." (KJV, Isaiah 66:1-2) I perceived this as, "Heaven is my thought (mindset), and the earth is my vehicle to spread light and love." You can be a catalyst for good or evil.

Your consciousness influences what information emerges from the Quantum Field. With all thoughts, observations, and actions, choose good. Bring more heaven to this earth. You are a vehicle of divine greatness in human form. The coherence between your heart and brain can create harmony, which creates waves of harmony affecting other energy fields around you. Your will or intention sets the flow of positive or negative energy into the Quantum Field. Your consciousness collapses the waves of probability into particles of creation. Your perspective creates a predisposition that influences your reality.

You know you can feel someone's energy. Imagine you are a student walking into Science class. You can sense the teacher is in a bad mood even though they haven't said anything yet. You are sensing their energy before they even say anything. The same is true for a parent or child. You can sense their energy—it's either positive, neutral, or negative. A friend of mine once said, "Your energy introduces you before you even speak." It's so true. Be cognizant of the energy you emit.

Don't get stuck in the density of defeat. It depletes your energy. Realize that you are a body of energy walking through life—either consciously or unconsciously. If unconscious, your program simply repeats what you are used to. It's stuck on the same frequency. If conscious, your energy flows where your attention goes.

When someone observes you, does it affect you energetically at some level? Of course, it does, because it's an outside influence or introduction of energy into your field. As counselors Dr. Christine Berger and Dr. Suzan K. Thompson state in their ACA Counseling Corner blog "Biofield Therapies," "The biofield is a large field of energy that surrounds and extends out from the body about eight feet. No part of the energy system is visible to the human eye, but the biofield can be felt with the hands, often through either pressure or temperature changes."[50] Your energy is everything. The sooner you become aware of this fact, you gain the ability to take control of your life. Jesus said, "On that day you will realize that I am in my Father, and you are in me, and I am in you."[51] God said, "I AM THAT I AM."[52] This was an attempt to show us our power in human form. It takes a profound teacher to put the words into perspective so our ever-so-evolving minds can understand the messages our ancient spiritual teachers were trying to get us to realize. The Buddha had a similar message. Look at the big picture. Notice that all religions worship a higher power. When you worship and believe in a higher power, you raise your vibration and connect to the infinite intelligence that unites us all. It's the highest form of energy, and we all share it. We really are all one within the vacuum of creation. From whichever perspective you view it, it's essentially your consciousness that gives consistent thought form or co-creates your personal reality. Your reality is a creation of your consciousness. Where you place your attention is where your energy is directed. "I AM, that I AM" is telling you that God is your consciousness—your intention and awareness. You are whatever you say you are, and your reality will reflect this.

Life is all about reflection, evolution, and growth. Every present moment is your opportunity to learn, believe in something greater, and choose. You have the ability to choose a different path anytime. Surround yourself with people who genuinely care about your wellbeing. Don't get caught up in drama or conflict. Think before you speak. Practice being present and come from a place of gratitude in all your interactions. It's really that simple. We just complicate this precious gift called life. We get lost in our struggles and resist change because it's uncomfortable. We allow the ego to over-analyze, doubt our abilities, worry ourselves sick, judge, criticize, and ultimately live in fear for most of our lives. What are we so afraid of?

Being different?
Being vulnerable?
Being uncomfortable?
Being alone?

Most of us are afraid of change or of being the first to do something different. It's uncomfortable. It's outside of the "normal." But we are living a "new normal." The catalyst has been introduced on a global scale, shifting our perspectives. Now is the time for you to put your perspective into focus, connect to your power, and go after your light. Courage is required to overcome our programs. Believe that you can shift the direction of your life and stop repeating the same patterns. Say this out loud: **"I Can... I Will... I AM!"**

Say, "I can live pain-free, I will live pain-free, I AM living without that pain." Claim it. If you are not dealing with pain, then replace that with what you want to do. My mantra is: "I can become a #1 Amazon Best-Selling Author and transformational speaker, I will become a #1 Amazon Best-Selling Author and transformational speaker, I AM a #1 Amazon Best-Selling

Author and transformational speaker!" I can make a difference in the world. I will make a difference in the world. I am making a difference in the world! We are here to learn how to evolve into a greater version of ourselves, escape from the ego's reign, rise above the limitations, awaken to our truth, power, and open the door to possibilities.

What is possible? Anything is possible when you **connect to your power**. Anything...

- ~ Flying planes.
- ~ Flying cars.
- ~ Blackberries.
- ~ FaceTime.
- ~ Google.
- ~ Holograms.
- ~ Apple Watch.
- ~ Neuro Feedback.
- ~ Heart Transplants.
- ~ eLearning.
- ~ Forgiveness.
- ~ Peace on Earth.

Don't be fooled by... the program... the stories you were told... the mass thinking we have all picked up along this journey...

- ~ Money doesn't grow on trees.
- ~ You aren't smart enough.
- ~ There isn't enough time.
- ~ You are too old.
- ~ Women can't be leaders.
- ~ You are stupid.
- ~ It will never work.

- ~ No one loves me.
- ~ I can't.
- ~ You will never amount to anything.
- ~ You are different, you won't fit in.
- ~ You are crazy.
- ~ If you don't go to college, you won't be successful.

Don't get stuck trying to live up to someone else's expectations or allow yourself to be brainwashed into believing you are unworthy or incapable of having a better life. This is your life and your soul's journey. Don't let the opinions or biases of others define your happiness or deplete your peace. Remember, whatever goes through your mind will manifest in your results.

> "What you choose to pay attention to is your consciousness under control and that intended awareness creates your reality."
> —Carrie L. Schmidt

The screen is a program—a system of inherited or learned patterns of thinking, beliefs, experiences, and excuses that are running your life on autopilot ninety-five percent of the time. It's your unconscious program. When you become aware of the SCREEN or the lens through which you view this lifetime, you have the ability to flip it. That paradox is like a reflection in the mirror. It's tricky. I dove into my subconscious programming to understand why the same patterns kept repeating in my life. It may be a continuous theme that shows up for you in your relationships, with your health, or in your profession. Those things that trigger a negative response in your mind and body. That longing or discontent has plagued you for too long. That thing you wish you could change… well, get ready to get excited about the future, because you can **change your program.**

BEHIND THE SCREEN

Exercise: Infinite Possibilities

Reflect on these questions in your *Life Timeline Journal.*

1. List today's date.
2. Now think and dream big. Dig deep down into your heart. What is possible for you? Your future? Your family?
3. If you did not allow the expectations and opinions of others to affect your decisions, what would you do differently?
4. What does peace feel like?
5. What does happiness look like? What is your soul longing for? What would you love?
6. What can you do, what will you do, what are you doing? (I can, I will, I AM...)

Chapter 9
Paradox of Perception

Step 4 – FLIP IT

> "*Progress is impossible without change,
> and those who cannot change their minds cannot
> change anything.*" [53]
> —George Bernard Shaw

A Course in Miracles says, "The world we see merely reflects our own internal frame of reference—the dominant ideas, wishes, and emotions in our minds. Projection makes perception."[54] We can portray how we view the outside world using the glass half-full/half-empty paradox, which describes polar opposite perspectives of life and situations. A pessimist sees the glass as half-empty, whereas an optimist sees the same glass as half-full. The screen is a metaphorical paradox which determines a viewer's reality. The side you view the screen of your life from reflects your results.

Human beings are wired to recall negative experiences because of our bodies' fight or flight nervous response. This allows our body to act instantaneously in order to survive when a past danger is presented again. It's important to flip our perspective on past situations. So far, I have shared positive memories from my childhood upbringing, along with negative memories and feelings.

There is always good with bad, as explained by the Principle of Polarity. Positive and negative energy exist, weaving our Universe together, while the sun and moon take turns influencing our circadian rhythms. Darkness cannot exist without light. Our bodies need balance, just like our planet does. It's a continuous dance of life, similar to a musical melody that rises and falls … or a heartbeat … or the breath of it all. When your mind, body, and soul are in balance and connected, it can feel like heaven on Earth. Meditation, various forms of yoga, and breathwork can help you get balanced. If you experience depression or anxiety, this means your brain/body may be imbalanced—and we know by this point in the book that your mind affects everything. As we apply these concepts to our *Life Timeline*, we become aware of our subconscious programming. Step 4 is about flipping your perspective or screen. Remove your "self" from the recollection and look at the situation from another person's perspective. German Physicist Max Planck is the first to be quoted as saying, "When you change the way you look at things, the things you look at change."[55] The silver lining will always present itself, but sometimes, you need to look for it—or shift your perspective to see it.

As we go back and reflect on our experiences, it's important to identify our perspective, then and now. Are you looking at a memory in your head, behind your screen, from a glass half-full or half-empty perspective? I invite you to flip your perspective to that of the other person in the situation. Allow yourself to recall this memory from the other person's standpoint or screen. For example, remember the story about my mother going out and getting a job and my father's reaction? There are two perspectives to view that situation from.

My father, on the one hand, was a good man. But he was stuck in his conditioned mind from his childhood upbringing—his father had been an old-fashioned, strict, pessimistic German who likely instilled a prejudice program in Dad. I'd never met my grandfather, but I'd heard stories about the way he belittled my grandmother and was hard on his children. My grandmother and grandfather came over on a boat from Germany and he worked while Grandma stayed home and took care of the kids. She never learned how to drive, because her role was to be at home. Of course, all this influenced Dad's screen and affected his relationship with Mom. I'm sure it was hard for him to fathom Mom going out and getting a job. His screen was exploiting his own insecurities and maybe even the language he heard his father use. His upbringing set his mind on repeat with fear and worry about what Mom was doing in a workplace with all men. (This issue affects many men and stresses many marriages in our world today.) Mom, on the other hand, responded by asking for a divorce. I'm sure she got tired of being screamed at every time she left the house or even wore a skirt. I can see their different perspectives.

Similarly, my ex, Trey, picked up generational conditioning. He was raised by his father, who cheated on his mother and stepmother. Then, he repeated that behavior in his life, which affected mine. We become fractals of our conditioning. The way we were raised has a profound impact on our mindset and behaviors throughout the rest of our lives, because our subconscious minds remember everything, even without our conscious awareness.

Here are some examples in which I applied Step 4—FLIP IT to my *Life Timeline*. Even though I've shared a lot of painful memories of my childhood, it wasn't terrible. What good came from these experiences? After my parents' divorce, when I was eight to eleven years old, I got to spend one-on-one time with Dad every other weekend. On Sundays, we'd spend all day watching football and bonding. Dad was the biggest Pittsburgh Steelers fan. To this day, I still bleed black and gold. Dad cooked the best pot roast (and usually burned it), but still, it was good. I loved Dad's cooking, along with his great big hugs and loving attention. He used to play his music real loud when he was getting ready to go out, and he'd spray on so much cologne you could smell him coming six blocks away. My dad was a cool dude with a funny personality. My sister, brother-in-law, Dad and I spent many quality Sundays together. We went boating, fishing, and camping and created a lot of great memories. I became extremely close with Kim and Jim, who would take me to motocross races and mudding in the woods. We'd have cookouts, parties, go camping, swimming, fishing, and take weekend trips to the mountains to ride four wheelers and snowmobiles. We had a blast. I cared about what Kim and Jim thought of me. They instilled a lot of the core values that define me today. I love them, and I'm grateful for the quality time we spent together before the teenage drama began.

So you see, it's important to look at the other side of life sometimes. While our survival mechanism may turn on without our awareness, we can train ourselves to notice its program or its unnecessary protection in our lives. We can flip it and override its control through our awareness of the paradox. Look for the brighter side—the laughter, the joy, and the lessons that taught us what we know now. Maybe there was a blessing that followed a past trauma or tragedy? There is always a silver lining... you just need to look for it.

When I look for the bright side, before the divorce, I realize that my mother was trying to do her best. She got pregnant with my sister at seventeen and married my father. They were kids, trying to manage a relationship. That takes work and communication. My father wasn't great at communication. That's the biggest weakness in most relationships (and even workplaces). After the divorce, she was trying to find herself and independence. It's difficult to raise a child on your own. I know this now! I was stubborn, rebellious. Almost all my struggles were a result of my own making. Each one taught me the lesson I needed to learn. You can't blame others for your problems or even your download, or subconscious programming, because that's a remnant of the past that needs to be recycled.

Whether it's flipping, releasing, or forgiveness, you need to do it. It is essential for your personal development. So, do it. Flip it. See it for what it is—a life lesson teaching you what your soul needs to progress through its journey in physical form.

> "If you don't make peace with your past, it will keep showing up in your present." [56]
> —Dr. Wayne Dyer

Exercise: Step 4 – FLIP IT:

Now, it's your turn. Recall the issues, triggers, or behavior patterns you tagged in step one. Then remember the earliest memory and feel the emotions you felt during that experience. Now Flip it. Look at the experience from a new screen, or perspective.

Reflect in your *Life Timeline Journal*...

~ What comes up for you when you apply Step 4?
~ What perspective are you able to see differently?
~ How do you feel when you see the story from the other side?
~ Is there a silver lining or something good that resulted from this experience?

Whatever you went through, it is in the past. You are in control now. You have the power because you are aware of your thoughts. Direct your thinking—how has the trauma you endured shaped you into becoming a better person?

Aren't you capable of so much more as a result? For example, perhaps when you were a child, you moved a lot, and that was hard. But because you learned to adapt quickly to new situations, you are now a versatile and resourceful adult. Sometimes it's difficult to flip the screen, because we still have so much pain bottled up in our energy bodies. Do your best. Take your time during this reflection. Your intuition will guide you through the paradoxical screen. Trust it and surrender to its infinite wisdom.

Change the Channel

Our stories and memories play on our movie screens, whether we are conscious of it or not. Sometimes they plague your mind, forcing you to seek some kind of escape. If you need to escape a way of thinking, apply Steps 1 – 4 and see what comes up. (Tag it, Remember it, Feel it, Flip it.) Figure out why this story is stuck on repeat. Get conscious and curious about why you feel the need to run away, get drunk, or eat another bag of potato chips. This could be your key to stepping into your truth and regaining control over yourself. Forget what those people said about you and reclaim your power. Maybe you're stuck on an embarrassing moment or a situation in which someone shamed you. Maybe you were teased or bullied as a kid, so you feel insecure. Whomever made you feel small, unwanted, or unloved could have been projecting their own internal conflicts onto you. Forget whatever negative story is playing behind your screen. Flip it. Tune into a new channel. Disrupt that voice in your head by taking a deep breath and quieting the chatter of its egoic influence. If you avoid situations because of a shameful event from your past, or worry about the future events that haven't yet happened... Stop. Simply detach yourself from that perspective. Just notice what you are noticing. Act as if you are an outsider viewing that story. What would the outsider see that you may not?

My story of a broken family has been on repeat and as long as I view it from that perspective, it will show up on my screen. I'm taking my power back and flipping my perspective to a new story: My family is not broken and neither am I. I am loved, complete, and open to receiving true love. I am successful and beginning a new chapter of life that will impact thousands of lives positively. My mother is a part of my son's life and mine; my friends are my family and are here to support me. If we need them, my brother-in-law and sister are always available. I have aunts and uncles who love Caysen and me and who would be happy to hear from us any time if we reached out. I shied away from my family long ago, never realizing it was me who ran away from them. I contributed to the brokenness of my story. Unconscious that my actions were hurting and affecting my family, I continued to believe they didn't love me when in reality they did—very much! That is why they were trying to protect me from the judgment and ridicule our society places on those who are different. The stereotypes that follow the African American population are real. They were trying to protect me from the heartbreak and agony of loving a man who didn't know how to love me back.

Once you become aware that your perspective has an impact on your reality, you will start to view the screen from many different angles. I was stuck on autopilot for the greater part of that nine-year relationship with Trey; stuck in a program where I thought his love completed me when in fact it was ripping my heart open. That void was growing like a black hole. As women, instead of feeling like we need a man, why don't we see our beauty within and value our "Self" more? Maybe my "need" came from not having a father when I needed one. This unconscious need shaped my decision-making as a teenager and followed me into adulthood. If my dad had been there to support me as a teenager (13 to 18 years old), maybe I wouldn't have stayed so many years in an unhealthy relationship. Who knows? Either way, it is irrelevant because we can't change the past. What matters is my perspective, so I can stop the pattern from showing up in my *Life Timeline* now and into the future. I can FLIP IT!

    I can only influence the present moment. I can flip my screen and delete the story of always feeling alone, unsupported, or unloved. If the story shows up, I notice it for what it is and then I flip it. I remind myself that, I don't need a man to be happy or feel loved. I don't need a man to take care of me. Self-love is the most important love there is. I can do this for myself. When you love yourself and feel complete as a spiritual being, you attract that "like energy." My unconscious behavior patterns were a programmed way of thinking and reacting based upon a past that no longer has control over me.

    Now I see the light and beauty of being loved and appreciated consciously. I can hug my mother and feel her love. She has been there for Caysen and me through thick and thin. She helped me raise him; I didn't do it alone. I am grateful for her support. I wish Caysen had had a father or a role model to help guide him along his journey, but I can't allow that void to cloud my screen or his. I can flip the screen and see a different perspective and outcome. I'm an amazing mother! Caysen and I have an unbreakable bond. The connection we share is so strong and loving. That shift alone changes my reality. I choose to look at the way people perceive me differently as well. People don't judge me; they admire my confidence and determination. They admire me. When I do this, I react differently with those people. I don't give them an attitude or look at them funny (because I think they are judging me). This viewpoint allows me to let down my walls. I'm able to share my stories and help other parents, teens, and young adults search for their truth and find balance, peace, and happiness. I'm open to sharing my life and love with a man, without fearing that he will cheat or break my heart.

It's critical to unravel the layers of conditioning to find your higher Self. Your truth. Your power. We carry energy with us from our past that gets re-energized every time our story makes an appearance on our screen. Whether it is your story of heartbreak or loss or my story of a broken family, it is connecting us to the vibrational frequency or energy from that time, thereby depleting the energy available in the present moment. Analyze the energy you have been holding on to. Where are you holding it in your physical body? You could have physical pain or chronic problems showing up because of this invisible force that needs to be cleared. Can you notice if your energy fluctuates within different environments or around certain people? Take note of your realizations. Write them down. Are you in control of your actions and conscious of your responses to others, or are you allowing your subconscious mind and body to run the show?

Set your soul free by detaching from the bonds of the egoic screen. When you do, you open up your energy field to infinite possibilities. Step into a new story with grateful expectation and a burning desire to see your **passion or purpose manifest.**

When the story on repeat in your head involves another individual, remember, there are two sides to every story. The stories we play in our head may not always be true. Over time, the facts may fade based upon the angle of your screen. Every person looks through their own screen. If you have unsettled family matters or have held on to anger or resentment for another person, it may be time to flip it and talk to them about your perspective and theirs to find the balance needed to repair the relationship for your sake, theirs, or your loved ones. They may have been living with unresolved resentment or stuck energy as well. Why not try to resolve it? You may not want to open Pandora's box, but you could have a life-changing conversation. It could be the key to getting your life or family back. Maybe it's the key to find your inner peace? Transformation takes root in your ability to be vulnerable, to surrender, and to let love lead the way. It's your choice. Your conscious attention and intention will deliver the best results throughout your *Life Timeline*.

I believe everything that has happened during my *Life Timeline* has happened for a reason. My life experience has given me a voice, taught me perseverance, and given me the faith to override fear and worry. I believe I learned how to overcome judgment, criticism, and heartbreak to teach other young women that they can escape the darkness as well. Maybe my soul was being prepared for a larger purpose? Maybe yours was, too? We will never know for sure, but we can rest in knowing that we have the will to connect to our power, gain clarity, and overcome the subconscious programming or past trauma that may be holding us back from serving our true purpose.

My soul has a purpose. Yours does, too! As long as you are diligent in the pursuit of your heart-felt passions, you will feel alive and expansive. Your vibrational frequency will rise, allowing you to connect with higher realms and infinite opportunities. Expand your mind, open your heart, and allow your soul to sing uplifting and expansive melodies. Your positivity will ripple through the Universe like a rainbow on steroids.

Chapter 10
Where There's a Will, There's a Way

The Beginning of the End

> "Normality is a paved road: it's comfortable to walk,
> but no flowers grow on it." [57]
> —Vincent van Gogh

I was free at twenty-three, enjoying every second of every day without a worry in my mind. When you release yourself from the bonds and expectations of other people, and just live for the day, it's exhilarating. I was single, had one year left of college, and partied like a Rockstar. Even though my friends and I partied hearty, I still got straight A's in college. That was always a personal achievement I needed to fulfill. In December 2005, I became the first person in my family to graduate from a four-year university—and I did it with honors. Of course, this was an accomplishment to celebrate. My friends and I did just that.

Soon after, I met Colt at a local bar while buying a group of my friends shots. He was standing next to me, so I politely offered to buy him and his friend a shot. We got to talking. He was living in a halfway house after recently getting out of jail on marijuana charges. That didn't bother me—remember, I was a 'misfit'. We hung out playing pool the rest of the evening and I met up with him the next day. For the next three months, we were inseparable. We fell in love. The way Colt wanted and needed me attracted me. I could help him. His childhood had been difficult, and he didn't have a family to support him, either. He was like me; lost in the program.

We attract the energy we project. As I look back, this reflection seems to be a reoccurring theme in my life. I am attracted to those who want or need me, but who also need some sort of healing. We can heal each other. However, I want to caution you about this repeating pattern. It is not healthy to need someone to heal you. At the same time, you shouldn't feel like you need to heal someone else. All healing must come from within. You must be complete and happy with yourself before anyone else can complete you. False expectations stem from faulty programs.

It had been two years since I'd left Trey. I was ready to give my love again and tired of going to bed alone every night. I moved into Colt's one-bedroom apartment and tried to have a loving relationship again. After three months, we got our own apartment and signed a year-long lease. We were planning a future. That's when I found out I was pregnant. I yearned for a family and someone to love me, unconditionally. It got real when I saw the evidence staring back at me on that pregnancy test stick. It overwhelmed me with excitement, wonder, and worry. We were excited and happy to be having our "Little Baby Bugg." My Hawaiian baby. Colt was half-Hawaiian and half-Irish. In the beginning, he took good care of me while I was pregnant. He did the cooking and cleaning, rubbed my belly, gave me massages, and rubbed my feet.

After my first ultrasound, I remember driving down the highway listening to the sonogram recording of the baby's heartbeat. I held the device up to my ear and played the recording over and over again—this tiny heartbeat of life, a life that would give me purpose. I immediately stopped smoking, drinking, and started focusing on my health for my baby. I tried to convince Colt to get on board with a positive lifestyle. That wasn't so easy. I filled out job applications for him, but he wouldn't go to the interviews. I begged him to change, but I knew from experience you can't change someone.

It was a tough pregnancy—constant fighting and stress between the two of us. There were some ugly fights. I was changing my life in preparation for becoming a mother and providing a stable environment for my baby. Colt continued selling and doing drugs. I tried to break up with him multiple times—once he pulled a gun on me and walked around our apartment like a maniac promising to kill me and my family if I left him. Once again, I asked myself, "What did I get myself into?"

I wanted to leave, but I was terrified of raising a child on my own. The last few weeks of my pregnancy, I was sleeping on my sister's couch with an enormous belly—it was extremely uncomfortable. I was living out of a suitcase, trying to prove something to Colt; trying to get him to understand that I would not raise my child in a terrible environment. I wouldn't fight with him anymore. It wasn't healthy for the baby. I didn't know what to do; I was so scared! I would have crazy dreams. I dreamed I was going into labor and I kept telling the doctors the baby wasn't ready to come out yet; it was too soon! They pulled him out anyway and surprise... he was a chicken with no feathers! I said to the doctors, "See, I told you he wasn't ready. Put him back in!" So they shoved the chicken with no feathers back inside me. I think it was me who wasn't ready. Your subconscious speaks to you in dreams.

I stayed with Colt hoping we could work it out... be a family. I didn't want to be a part of another "Broken Family!"

I was working as a Marketing Director for a chiropractor while pregnant, and I went into labor while at work, three weeks early. The day had come to meet my angel baby.

The Breath of Life

The seed planted in my belly was a blessing in disguise. It gave my life meaning and purpose. My son saved my life. Caysen Ray Schmidt, you were my awakening. There is nothing that can compare to the unconditional love I feel for you. You are my reason for being—for breathing. I talked to you in my belly and sang you sweet melodies—my chicken without feathers—and we said prayers together once you were old enough to talk. I will never forget those sweet words spoken by the green plush stuffed animal that became our prayer buddy every night before bed. We would all say, "Now I lay me down to sleep. I pray the Lord my soul to keep, as the angels watch me through the night until I wake in morning light."

BEHIND THE SCREEN

The love of my life; my Baby Bear!

Caysen,

Your birth awakened my heart and soul, like a shooting star brightens up the night sky. They overflow with so much abundant and infinite love for you always and forever. You showed me what unconditional love is. God planted you inside my belly for a reason. You are special in so many ways. Creative. Funny. Intelligent. Spiritual and Compassionate. I love you more than any word could ever express. You opened my eyes to a whole new world. You brought so much light into my life when I had none. Thank you for helping me grow into the woman I am today. I look forward to watching you grow into an amazing, loving, and confident man.

Infinitely grateful to be your Mama! I love you!

Mama

That cold winter Wednesday in December at the Sharon Regional Hospital was a pivotal point on my *Life Timeline*. It was like standing in the end-zone when the stadium lights come on. My complete energy-being absorbed the biggest photon of light energy when Caysen was placed on my lap. When our eyes met, my heart overflowed with so much love and gratitude. My first wake-up call. This innocent soul was now my responsibility to care for and provide for. My heart beat for him; he became my purpose. His eyes were the doorway to an unexplainable soul connection between the two of us. They say, "Love is more precious than gold." Well, I became a millionaire Mom on December 13, 2006. The lightbulb turned on inside my head! This child revived my heart and repaired my soul. He gave me a reason to breathe and want to strive to thrive, instead of simply survive. Seasons of darkness can deliver you two lifetimes of delight—in one split second. I went from being so dark, lost in fake love, and surviving the depths of depression, to yearning for something greater and then receiving a miracle of nativity. Thank you, God. I got my chicken with feathers! A blessing of life—he opened my heart, restored the blood flow and enabled my spirit to come back to the surface.

My soul was saved by a tiny six-pound, seven-ounce gift from God. That's how the Universe works. The light was so bright, it shone all the fear away. I wasn't afraid to do anything anymore. I had a reason to live; I could conquer the world. This was the beginning of my transformation. I would go after my dreams and turn my life around for my son. My entire way of thinking, feeling, and acting changed overnight. Isn't it funny how our lives can take such a drastic turn? Like the saying goes, "The Lord works in mysterious ways!" I don't think it's funny, ironic, or a mystery. It's the work of the almighty Creator—it's the spirit of God. It's the work of the great I AM! When you are at your worst, you can be saved. The essence of light reminds you of who you are.

Before all the programming, I was conscious of my superpowers. I described them with vivid detail when I wrote and illustrated my first book about Shelia Bedelia in first grade. Shelia was a superhero woman with a vision to see beyond limitations. She planted seeds of greatness and watched them grow into life-changing miracles. I've had the vision and power since six years of age. Maybe Shelia Bedelia was a vision of my future self, who is now writing this book.

I connected back to my power as I held my newborn baby in my arms. I have the power to override the programs conditioned from my past. I am aware of the light our world needs. Now my screen is clear—the black fog that once blurred my screen is gone. I have vision and power. I am in control. The future will look different. Creating goals and taking action is easier now that I have a purpose. I have someone greater than myself to care for. This energy and awareness of unconditional love can conquer kingdoms and blossom the most bountiful miracles.

Colt and I brought Caysen home from the hospital in his blue Carebear snowsuit, and he never left my side. I tried to make our family unit cohesive, but Colt wasn't stable. Caysen and I needed stability. I went through a few months of postpartum depression. I knew we were going to leave and do this on our own, but it took two months for me to build up the courage.

An Energetic Detox

(Side Note: I haven't recalled these memories or shared this story with anyone for more than thirteen years, so it's painful to relive the memories of struggle and despair as I write this story). This work is required to complete the *7-Step Life*

Timeline System of Transformation. The trigger is tagged. Now I have to remember it, feel it (now), flip it, and then apply Step 5 – Release It. I will do this NOW, release the repressed emotions from the past.... WOW, I just realized it is 8:21 p.m. on 8/21/2020—I'm attaching the picture below to showcase this genuine moment of awareness in time as I type these words on my computer.

ACTUAL MOMENT IN TIME

The Universe speaks to us in infinite ways, sometimes through symbols, signs, or mathematics. They say mathematics is the language of the Universe. I'm interested to learn what this sequence of numbers means in numerology: 8212020. So, I googled. According to *angelnumber.org*, "...the angel number 821 is a message from your guardian angels, asking you to maintain a positive outlook on the future. This number announces you are close to manifesting the desired abundance in your life."[58] WOW....

BEHIND THE SCREEN

As I relived these memories in my mind and felt the emotions in my physical body, I became conscious of this number (date and time—in real time). It was a sign that it's OK. It's OK to remember it, feel it, flip it, and finally release it. This system of transformation is necessary for my soul to continue its journey. This is meant to be. I have guardian angels summoning me to continue... continue to be aware... continue to proceed... continue to choose the path I am on... and to manifest transformation in my life, my son's life, and others' lives. "I can, I will, I am!" I did it then and I can do it now. This is a process, and it takes effort to overcome painful reflections of the past. The real work is releasing the energy that's followed me for too many years. I will apply Step 5 – Release It.

CARRIE'S LIFE TIMELINE EXAMPLE
Applying Steps 1 - 5
Write it down and pin it up on your Life Timeline, the day you "tagged it."

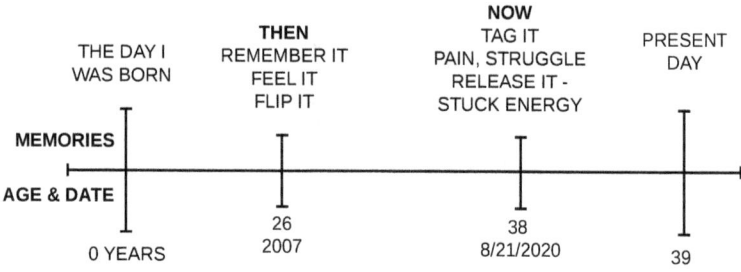

I will continue sharing my story with you. At the end, we will reflect on my realizations and release the energy that's been stuck in my subconscious.

Colt and I argued and fought about everything. I knew it wasn't healthy, nor would it get any better. It was time to leave. It would be difficult. I asked myself, "Am I making the right choice? Can I do this alone?" I analyzed every decision in the smallest detail until it drove me crazy. I had to find my power, connect to it, ask for Universal guidance, and act.

It was a cold, gray day in Ohio when I dressed Caysen in his blue Carebear snowsuit, packed the diaper bag full, and went to leave for good. But Colt wouldn't let me go. He was on some kind of drug and acting weird. We argued. He wrestled with me while I was holding Caysen. I didn't want to fight. We were both crying. My poor baby was stuck in the middle of this energy and experiencing this struggle—even babies can sense conflict. It affects their wellbeing—recall the delta and theta state of consciousness their brain operates within. After fighting, crying, and trying to escape, I finally got Caysen in the car. As I was backing down the driveway, Colt ran after the car. He threw a brick at my passenger side door. My entire body was shaking as I backed into the street and put the car into drive. Then he jumped on the hood of my car and hung on to the windshield wipers as I tried to drive down the street. It was insane; I could not believe it was happening! I don't remember him getting off the hood, but I got away.

I had nowhere to go. I escaped to my mom's workplace to decide on our next step, just me and my newborn baby. I had to file a police report that day against him—I was afraid for our safety. He was slightly crazy. I don't remember where I went or how long we stayed away, but of course, he made me feel bad, and I went back. I tried. I cared. I wanted our family to work out. I felt bad for Colt so I gave him every opportunity to make our family work. It didn't. I had to leave.

Now, can you see the pattern? A broken family? I tried. I felt bad—for us all. I had to muster up the confidence to walk away—again. Do we create our own realities based on our subconscious program? Do we repeat the same behaviors—within different relationships? Do we attract the same type of people or situations into our life? Will we wake up from the illusion?

A few weeks later, I had another chance to leave. It was so scary, but necessary. Nothing had changed. I knew it never would. After wasting nine years in an unhealthy relationship—expecting the other person to change... well you and I both know the outcome. I decided, "This is my chance." Colt left with a friend, probably to make a drug deal. It was a cold, dark evening in February. I raced to pack my black Chevy Cavalier with as much of our stuff as I could fit in it before he came back. I planned to come back another day with my sister and friends to gather the rest of my furniture and belongings. The coast was clear, so I had to escape while I had the chance. With about twenty dollars to my name, Caysen and I got in the car and drove away from the home I had been so hopeful about living in as a family. The only person that could change Colt was Colt. I tried to help. That is all that matters, in my opinion. My son deserved so much better. Intuitively, I knew we would be better. I acted with faith and overruled the fear and doubt that tried so hard to hold me back. I believed in a future that held endless opportunities and countless blessings for Caysen and me.

We moved into my dad's two-bedroom apartment. Caysen and I shared a small room with my queen bed, his crib, and about a four-foot by four-foot space to stand. We made it work, because we needed little—just each other. Just looking into his eyes and seeing him smile brightened up ten lifetimes a day. I shared so many priceless memories with my son and my father during this time. We grew so much closer and I believe this was our opportunity to re-connect. My Dad was so great with Caysen; he loved him so much. "Monkey Boy!" he called him. I loved watching them bond and play together. Caysen loved his Papa. As I look back now, this time allowed Caysen, my dad, and me time to bond and cultivate a loving connection.

You're probably wondering what happened to Colt, right? I still couldn't tell you. It's a mystery how someone can give up and not even try to be a father. Kim, Jim, and their friends went back to the house to help me get all my furniture and belongings. Thankfully, Colt was not there. He did stick me with the last month's rent and bills since they were in my name. He came to Dad's apartment two weeks later to see Caysen. When I asked him for some money, he reluctantly handed me a twenty-dollar bill, saying that's all he had. That was the ONLY money I ever received from that man. It was the last time we saw him. After that, he was incognito, and I was moving forward with our life!

Today, as a 38-year-old, successful, confident woman, I look back over those memories of being a twenty-six-year-old, brand-new mother. I remember how I felt at that time—afraid, alone, determined. I had a longing for more—a yearning in my soul to do better. An innocent child needed me. Caysen needed me to love him unconditionally. I had to provide and care for him. I couldn't rely on anyone else to make that happen. I had to flip my perspective from that negative situation with Colt to adopt a positive outlook and create a future filled with laughter, joy, and peace. I realize I am still carrying the weight of this past life in my energy body at thirty-eight years old and it feels heavy. I tucked it away long ago and forged a new path, trying as hard as I could to never look back. We succeeded, Caysen and I. However, the unprocessed, bottled-up energy still resides. I choose to release that energy from my energy body now. I must physically release it. I say out loud, "I forgive you, Colt, for not being there for Caysen and me all these years." I forgive myself for leaving because I knew it was the best decision for our future. These are methods for clearing emotional blocks or releasing stuck energy that I will explain further in the following chapter. Right now, I am using journaling (through writing the stories in this book) to help release the energy of my past with Colt. Through my writing, I can release the energy. At the same time, I am also incorporating breathing and meditation into this release. I close my eyes and focus on the power breathing me. I connect to this power and feel its warmth and love in each of my 50 trillion cells. I allow it to cleanse my spirit and detox my body. I express gratitude for this release and offer the energy to the Universe for recycling. It feels good to release those unprocessed emotions from my past consciously so I can continue to focus on and manifest a fulfilling future.

Colt was not a bad person. He had a good heart. As a child, he had lost his power to severe abuse and family abandonment. He'd never gained it back. He got stuck in that subconscious program, trying to escape the pain of the past with drugs. It's sad how destructive that program can be. Even after everything I've been through, I forgive him. I pray for him to find peace and happiness.

Forgiveness is one of the most powerful decisions you can make. Releasing resentment for (or anger about) another person frees your soul by cleansing those feelings of stuck energy. This form of energetic release will allow your being to open up and attract higher vibrational experiences. You can let go and seek understanding or empathy, which opens you up **for greater things**.

Chapter 11
Releasing Repressed Emotions

Step 5 – RELEASE IT

> "Unexpressed emotions will never die.
> They are buried alive and will come forth later in uglier ways." [59]
> —Sigmund Freud

Welcome to Step 5 of the *Life Timeline System of Transformation.*

The research of two renowned experts has proven that repressed emotions can factor into medical health conditions such as stress, anxiety, or depression. Dr. Candace Pert, an internationally recognized neuroscientist and pharmacologist who published over 250 research articles and wrote the book *Molecules of Emotion*,[60] explains how our thoughts and emotions affect our health. Dr. Bradley Nelson, an energy healer, author (*The Emotion Code®: How to Release Your Trapped Emotions for Abundant Health, Love, and Happiness*),[61] and creator of The Body Code™ System, believes we can heal past trauma and release trapped emotions with his system of energy healing.

Remember the mental health statistics we explored earlier? Imagine for a second how many people are hiding behind their screen, suffering. Think about how many women are stuck in unhealthy relationships, dealing with abuse, afraid to leave because they don't have anywhere to go. The screen shades their true power and depletes their passion. These women are forced to live a lie and hide their misery behind a fictitious lens. When we hide or bottle up negative emotions, they become stuck in our energy body. Illness takes root in our energy body before it manifests as a physical symptom. According to an *International Journal of Psychotherapy Practice and Research* article, "Consequences of Repression of Emotion: Physical Health, Mental Health and General Well Being," "The

RELEASING REPRESSED EMOTIONS

ways in which humans manage their emotions has become one of the most important but least examined concerns in medicine today.... When poorly managed or regulated, they [emotions] can lead to negative health and psychological consequences."[62] Repressed emotions can lead to physical symptoms such as muscle pain and tension, nausea and digestive problems, fatigue, and sleep problems. Unresolved anger can have significant health consequences and can lead to higher risk for developing high blood pressure, digestive issues, and cardiovascular disease.[63] These problems can fester for years until they turn into weeds. Let's get rid of those weeds and fertilize your soil for greatness!

Reflecting on my *Life Timeline*, I suppressed and bottled up many negative emotions to survive. I stopped crying after years of getting my heart broken by Trey. The tears were drowning me and no one was coming to the rescue. Only you can save yourself—it's through your consciousness that you gain power. I didn't have anyone to teach me or guide me in this process. I got by, day by day. I wiped my eyes, looked in the mirror and said, "Suck it up, Carrie! Get your mind right. Stop being vulnerable and open. Shut down your heart. Stop caring!" Shutting my heart off from feeling was the way to stop the pain. Just as our brains need practice to move a memory from short to long-term storage, I trained my mind to stop dwelling and my heart to stop caring. I threw in the towel, left the relationship, stayed away, and stopped wishing for a different outcome. The problem is, I didn't process the emotions or release the energy properly. The energy from each broken relationship followed me and lingered in my being. It hid behind my screen. The invisible walls I built around my heart withheld those suppressed emotions while I tried to drown them with alcohol.

Slowly, I turned off the feeling and focused on my freedom. After enduring the shame and disappointment in my relationships with Trey and Colt, I turned into a runner. I cut people out of my life to avoid letting them hurt me. "Lose my phone number" was a tagline of mine that I delivered to countless men. If I got a clue that they'd lie, cheat, or hurt me, I cut them off. "Fuck off" was another one. Friends of mine often referred to this unconscious behavior pattern as my "switch." It was short and to the point. I knew that I had the power to overcome any circumstance by now, so why would I ever waste my time on someone who wasn't serious about me? My time is precious, and my energy is my strength; waste either and I leave. I walked away—from relationships, opportunities, and friendships. Ironically, that survival mechanism will only isolate you more. Over time, isolation turns into loneliness and depression. What I thought I needed to survive was killing my ability to be happy and find love later on.

Methods of Energy Release

It's time to release whatever emotions you bottled up and shoved down deep into your being. (This step should be done after you have already completed Tag It, Remember It, Feel It, and Flip It. Also, this step is most effective with professional support.) It's time to allow your emotions from the past to come up so you can properly process them and get them out of your system. Uproot its bonds by releasing the energy from your biofield and recycling it into the Universe. Those emotions need to be expressed and released. Here are some ways to release energy or repressed emotions:

Hypnotherapy
Hypnotherapy is a type of mind-body intervention in which a trained practitioner uses hypnosis to create

a state of focused attention and increased suggestibility in the treatment of a medical or psychological disorder or concern. When you enter a hypnotic state, you can explore painful thoughts, feelings, and memories you may have hidden from your conscious mind. This allows you to access your subconscious mind and release negative emotions while altering your level of consciousness. You feel like you are in the experience from your past and you can override that memory.

    I've been through several one-hour hypnotherapy sessions with therapist Liz Burkholder, who runs Burkholder Wellness in Charlotte, NC. She helped me access memories and repressed emotions from my past that I wasn't even conscious were still an issue for me. In just one hour, I remembered past traumas, felt the emotions, released them, and healed the broken child inside me. Hypnotherapy is a highly effective treatment for dealing with and healing painful experiences.

Awareness and Breathwork
Focused breathing can help restore balance to the systems of the body. There are various techniques that help you breathe to heal all levels of pain. The goal is to become aware of your breathing, control it, and allow any thought to just pass by your mind. Place your attention on the part of your body that is holding the pain. Breathe into that place deeply, and with each exhalation of your breath, set a clear intention to release that tension or stuck energy. Continue this exercise while you feel the painful energy exit your

body. You can even incorporate an audible tone as you express the energy through your out-breath. Focused breathing helps to turn off your monkey mind and hone in on your internal spiritual power and connection to Source. It helps you access higher dimensions outside our physical realm.

Journaling
Writing your memories, reflections, and emotions out on paper is a form of release. It provides an opportunity to identify negative thoughts, feelings, and behaviors. While you write, you allow those emotions to surface so you can release them consciously. You may incorporate positive self-talk and affirmations into your journaling process. It can also be helpful to burn the paper ritually and offer the ashes to the winds.

Tapping
Emotional Freedom Technique—or EFT—also known as tapping, is a self-healing technique that focuses on psychological issues by working with energy channels in the body. EFT uses the principles of acupressure, an ancient technique used to clear blockages along the meridians of the body by applying pressure to certain points. Do this with the tap of your finger anytime you feel stressed. Dr. Dawson Church, a health and science writer who has been researching, practicing, and teaching EFT for decades, said that,

> We are energy beings... Energy flows through the body and it flows in these channels. When we tap on our acupressure points, that produces a calming

piezoelectric signal that travels through our tissue to the source of our stress and rapidly calms it down.[64]

When you recall a traumatic event from the past, your brain kicks into fight or flight, but when you tap, you are telling your brain it's OK. Tapping helps to release energy and calm your central nervous system.

Crying

Crying helps to detoxify the body and restore emotional balance. According to an article in Healthline.com, "Crying for long periods of time releases oxytocin and endogenous opioids, otherwise known as endorphins. These feel-good chemicals can help ease both physical and emotional pain. Once the endorphins are released, your body may go into somewhat of a numb stage."[65] If you cry, you are not weak (as society makes us believe). In fact, you are expressing emotion in a healthy way instead of bottling it up.

Movement

Dance, exercise, yoga, tai chi, or any other form of motion helps release emotion. You allow your blood to flow, oxygen to move, and muscles to work, all of which increases endorphins. This is a very healthy way to release energy and make you feel good. I always feel amazing after one hour of physical exercise. Overrule your habitual mind if it says, "I'm too tired or I don't have enough energy." Movement gives you energy. It allows you to release stagnant energy and absorb satisfying stimulation. Singing is also a form of expressive movement that helps release energy.

Meditation

Meditation has been practiced for thousands of years as a type of mind-body complementary medicine. This powerful practice allows you to focus your attention on your breath in and out of your chest without engaging in the stream of thoughts that come up in your mind. It helps produce a deep state of relaxation through focused breathing. Meditation brings your mind and body into a state of balance and reduces stress. It also enhances working memory and executive function in the brain. There are various forms of meditation. You can find guided meditation audio and videos to help you with the practice from the comfort of your home or get professional support. Dr. Joe Dispenza has conducted extensive research to prove the healing powers of meditation. One such study published by Elsevier Ltd on behalf of the International Brain Research Organization concludes, "Findings suggest that brief guided meditation intervention may offer positive and immediate health benefits to help combat stress."[66]

I became acquainted with Mindfulness and Meditation during my first trip to San Diego, CA during a Lean Manufacturing conference. In a breakout session, organizers gathered attendees into one room. We were instructed to close our eyes, place both feet flat on the floor, and focus on our breathing: in and out, in and out. If a thought passed through our minds, we were advised to not interact with it, just to notice it and allow it to pass. The intention was to clear our minds and simply focus on our breathing.

After the twenty-minute session, I was amazed. I felt calmer, grounded, and clear-headed. After the conference, I continued the meditation practice at home. Each day, the practice got easier as I settled more into my body, calmed my overactive mind, and focused on the breath of life. It's a powerful practice that helps reduce anxiety, improve concentration, and restore balance within your energy body.

Forgiveness

We touched briefly on this concept earlier. The Christian saint, Augustine of Hippo, is quoted as saying, "To withhold forgiveness is to take poison and expect the unforgiven to die."[67] The only person suffering from your lack of forgiveness is you, because you continue to carry that energy of resentment, betrayal, or anger. It stays in your biofield until you decide to release it through the power of forgiveness. Put an end to blaming the other person for your pain. It doesn't mean you forget or excuse the harm done to you, but you release its bonds over you. First, you must decide to forgive, then follow a process. There are support groups, coaches, and counselors that can help guide you. American actor Tyler Perry said, "It's not an easy journey to get to a place where you forgive people. But it is such a powerful place, because it frees you."[68] Free yourself from bitterness, resentment, regret, guilt, and grievance. Let go of the grudges or anger and free your mind, body, and soul to resonate with higher vibes.

American social psychologist James W. Pennebaker and his colleagues performed research in 1997 which "demonstrated that individuals who repress their emotions also suppress their body's immunity, making them more vulnerable to a variety of illnesses ranging from common colds to cancer."[69]

Once your consciousness understands that holding on to this energy is not necessary; your energetic detox will be much easier. Cleanse your soul, knowing that your higher power is going to expel that energy and transform it into good. Afterwards, your vibration will rise and you'll be receptive to a new way of thinking as you enter into Step 6 – Reprogram.

Exercise: Step 5 – RELEASE IT

Use your *Life Timeline Journal* to reflect on the following questions:

~ Do you have repressed emotions lingering from your past or unprocessed energy that needs to be released? Can you identify where this stuck energy may be residing in your body? Do you have physical pain or symptoms as a result?
~ Which form(s) of Energy Release will you commit to trying?
~ When will you commit to do the Energy Release?
~ Do you feel like you need help or support from a friend or professional? If so, who will you call on?

Chapter 12
Life Happens Between the Rise and Fall of it All

A Fresh Start

> "Life will give you whatever experience is most helpful for the evolution of your consciousness..." [70]
> —Eckhart Tolle

Caysen and I settled into our new life together, and I started looking for a career. The problem was it would have cost more to put Caysen in daycare than I would have been paid (or at least I would only break-even). That didn't make sense, so I stayed home for seven months and spent one-to-one quality time with my bundle of joy. I breastfed him for his optimal health. We went for walks in the park, and hung out, laughing and playing. He was my buddy! Looking back, this time was priceless. I was gaining my confidence and character back. When you become a first-time mother, it's like being born again. That's a huge transition on your *Life Timeline*. I was a twenty-six-year-old single mother, broke, living with my father. On the other side of my screen was a bright future, where I would never have to worry about money. That long gravel road would be getting paved to make my path clear.

I searched for opportunities and took action steps every single day to move our life forward. That meant going to the government offices to get cash help, WIC, food stamps, and healthcare insurance. It was embarrassing to go through a grocery store checkout with WIC—the people behind you change lines because it takes forever to process those transactions. It was like wearing a big red badge that said, "Hi, I'm poor." I went to churches to get donations of clothes for Caysen. My friends gave me hand-me-downs, which also helped. I started going to counseling to process the experiences from my past and get clarity. That helped, too. I had to support myself and

Caysen. I was determined to provide the best life for him possible. It wasn't easy, but friends and family helped. Nothing that's worthwhile is easy.

With the will to grow, a purpose, and a fire in my soul, I continued applying for jobs. One day, I got a call from the HR Manager at CCL Container inviting me to interview for a Customer Service position I had applied for. I was so excited. This was a big company with excellent pay and benefits. I went to the interview and met with the Plant Manager and VP of Sales. It was incredible to see this gigantic aluminum can manufacturing facility in my hometown of Hermitage, PA. I had no idea that place even existed. As a child, I can remember driving by this large manufacturing plant on Swamp Road, wondering what they did there. I never knew they made the aluminum cans we use daily for hairspray, mousse, and sunscreen. I wanted that job! I learned in a college career prep course that you should always ask for the job if you want it. After all, it's the quality of questions you ask that will become the quality of your results in life. So, during my interview, I asked for the job. After the interview, I emailed a thank-you letter to the Plant Manager and waited. I prayed. Then I got the offer. The starting salary was more than the cut-off for childcare financial help. With financial assistance, I paid sixty dollars per week for childcare. Without it, I had to pay $600 per week. It made sense to make a couple thousand dollars less per year to get that benefit. I negotiated my starting salary down and began my employment.

This job turned into a career that would change my life. I was dedicated to succeeding. I devoted the next three years to my son and my career. I had no time for anything else. My focus and attention were clear. It's funny, because when training with the CSR Manager, I looked like a deer in headlights. She was explaining how to process a P.O. "What's a P.O.?" I asked. She looked at me like I was crazy. This young girl, with a newborn baby, straight out of college, training for an important position. A few years after I got hired, the plant manager told me some people said I was "too green," that in hiring me, he had made a mistake. He said, "I knew you were a diamond in the rough!" I said, "You hit the nail on the head." I am so grateful for the opportunity that Plant Manager gave me, because it had a profound impact on my ability to be the sole provider for my family. I never wanted to need anything from anyone.

For the first few years on the job, I was a sponge: feed me knowledge, share your experience, and enlighten me with information about the process. I wanted to learn HOW to make it better. I went out on the production floor to learn more. I ventured down to the front office to spend time with the VP of R&D, the VP of Engineering, and other department heads so I could listen to their stories. I asked a lot of questions. It was my way of gaining a better understanding of the entire process. I didn't realize how far this would take me in my career. I learned quickly and gained the confidence to speak up and ask questions when no one else would. I didn't take "no" or "I don't know" for an answer. I asked "Why?" a lot. Remember that eight-year-old genius (as my sister used to call me)? She was now a twenty-six-year-old genius in disguise. I would ask, "Why did that happen? Why don't we do it this way? Why don't we move this order over to another production line and group for efficiency?" I had been born with a brain focused on continuous improvement and it was really paying off. Soon, I had enough money to trade in my 1997 Chevy Cavalier for a brand-new red Pontiac G6. Caysen was enrolled in the best daycare in the valley, and I signed a lease for our own apartment. Life was coming together.

Everyday Evolution

We evolve every single day. We stumble and fall, learn and recall. Every day is an opportunity to grow. Improve. Change. Consciousness, or your awareness of existence and power in every present moment, is the secret. It allows you to escape from the program; your gift is the present moment. In the stillness of silence and magnitude of awareness, being mindful of your subconscious program allows you to be in control. Whatever life throws at you, through your consciousness, you can think before acting. Listen to your intuition and rise above the density of darkness. Because life happens between the rise and fall of it all.

Life Happens Between the Rise and Fall of it All:
Between the sunrise and sunset,
every breath in and out of your chest,
your first and last kiss.
Between every heartbeat and the words you speak.
Life happens between the rise and fall of it all,
From the waves of probability to the particles of creation,
it happens based on your observation.
Birthdays, graduations, and funerals,
love gained and love lost.
Resentment.
Opportunity cost.
It's a paradoxical perspective,
between your point of view and mine.
Life flies by in the blink of an eye.
From betrayal to forgiveness,
or choosing to honor your fear over faith.
Whether it's a paved or gravel road,
you decide the direction you go.
Either way,
Life happens between the rise and fall of it all.

Life was happening to Caysen and me between doctor's appointments, Emergency Room trips, ambulance rides, and hospital stays. For the first two years of his life, Caysen had a hard time breathing. The doctors couldn't tell me why. I didn't know what to do. My angel baby's face would turn blue. Countless doctors and specialists didn't have an answer. "Just take the medication prescribed," they'd say. Albuterol, steroids, nebulizer treatments. He had to do breathing treatments every six hours for an entire year. I sat in my bedroom, rocking him, while holding the nebulizer mask over his precious, round face. I stared into his innocent brown eyes, sharing loving energy while he breathed in the medicine to help open up his airways. This was not an easy time. Maybe God had been preparing me all along for this journey?

On day two of my employment, while I was still experiencing the stress of learning a brand-new job, Caysen was rushed to Pittsburgh Children's Hospital with breathing problems. They hooked him up to several machines monitoring his oxygen levels, heartbeat, and vitals. I was in the middle of training for my new job. They considered me "green" while my son was turning blue—all the colors of the rainbow. Life happens between the rise and fall of it all. Moments. Workdays. Hospital trips. Caysen's health condition terrified me because the doctors didn't have a solution.

Thank God Mom was there to help me. As much as I have resented her at times in my life, I am grateful for her. Mom has always been my constant, as I have been hers. Even though my family disowned me, my mother didn't. She was able to see beyond the skin color and support me to the best of her ability, even with all the critics on the other side scrutinizing her for it. She wasn't happy with the situation, but she didn't abandon me. She did the best she could to support me—even though I didn't see it from that perspective as a teenager. I see it now as a mother myself. Mom has always helped me with Caysen as well. We do not always see eye to eye, probably because of our screens. We hold people to certain expectations that can lead to disappointment. Unfortunately, that has always been an issue for us. "Mommies tend to become punching bags for their children," as my hairdresser uniquely pointed out to me. My expectations may be higher at times (my mom could do more), but I'm applying "the screen" to every viewpoint to help bridge the gap. It can be difficult for some people to see a different point of view (other than their own) and that keeps them stuck repeating the same results. As I came to realize this, I started to flip the screen, shifting my subconscious program over to manual so I could make better choices.

There is no guidebook for parenting. It's the hardest but most rewarding job on the planet. You never know how hard single parenting can be until you do it yourself. When Caysen was a baby, I was just trying to survive. We made countless trips to the Emergency Room. I spent days and nights trying to console him. Breathing treatments around the clock. The fear was the worst part. I had to turn off the tears and block the pain from stabbing my heart to death. I had to provide. I worked fifty hours a week. I took care of Caysen, the housework, the bills, and everything else that comes with life. I gave him as much love and attention as I could. He didn't have anyone other than me and Mom, and that always troubled me as a problem I couldn't solve. I couldn't provide him with a father. This ripped my heart apart, not just because I had to do it all alone, but I knew one day he would feel unresolved emptiness—a void. My pain was projected into silence and solidarity. I was alone and weak with worry, but my spirit empowered me to rise above it all because I had to. No one else would save us.

We saw pulmonologists, gastroenterologists, and countless other specialists to determine why Caysen had so much trouble breathing. The pure love that overflowed from my heart for him gave me the strength to make it through. Caysen was the light leading the way in my life (and always has been since that day our eyes first met). Thankfully, we found the solution to his breathing problems—they were caused by GERD (Gastroesophageal Reflux Disease).

Caysen's beautiful charm, contagious laugh, and enormous heart united my "broken" family and drew it back together. On his first birthday, Mom, Dad, my sister, brother-in-law, family, and friends all showed up to celebrate his birth and all his firsts. What a beautiful event—it was a time to remember. After seventeen years, my parents sat in the same room together. Caysen showed us all that the simplest ray of sunshine can transform seeds into flowers. The simplest gesture of love can withstand hurricanes of hurt. Holding on to the energy of the past will only reinforce that energy in your current life. My angel baby changed it all for me. He connected me to a love so much greater than anything in our finite world. With my focus fully directed on him, I didn't hold on to the resentment I felt for my family. I was just happy to have them back in my life again. They were there to support and love Caysen and I. That's what we needed. It all worked out.

Everything exists within your state of mind, and seeing things from a different perspective can be your saving grace. So, allow the grace of this day to save you. Apply Step 4—Flip It to flip the script in your head and view the blessings instead of the condemnation. Maybe life would have been a trillion times worse if Colt had remained in the picture. I could have ended up in jail or dead if Caysen hadn't been born. Don't get stuck on the same perspective. You are more powerful than your worst day. You will struggle in life, but you will always find a way. Billions of people are struggling between the rise and fall of something. The mountains may be high, but you have the power to climb them. Reach for the sky and enjoy the ride back down. The ups and downs, highs and lows, hills and valleys will never fade. Life happens between the rise and fall of it all! Allow your spirit to lead the way through your life and choose love in every interaction you can.

The Struggle is Real

On the second day of Caysen's stay in Pittsburgh Children's Hospital, as I sat there with my heart ripping apart, praying for my baby's lungs to open up, my Mom received a phone call that drove a rivet through both our souls. My uncle Danny, my godfather, had shot himself in the head with a 12-gauge shotgun. His wife found him dead outside in his truck. The week prior, he had come to visit me and Caysen at Dad's apartment. I never saw Mom's face look so horrified—her heart shattered. Tears poured down her face. Maybe, in Uncle Danny's mind, through his screen, a bullet in the head was less painful than living another day.

If we want to make this world a better place, we need to focus on mental health. Too many people suffer *Behind the Screen*. The mind, body, soul connection is the most powerful tool on the planet. But if you don't know this, you can get stuck in ego-driven ways of separation. The ego wants you to forget about your divine connection to Source. It strives to keep you competing for more, comparing yourself to others, and isolated in your despair. Life will continue to happen between the hours on the clock, relationships, hardships, and triumphs. God will try to get your attention through the softest sign, powerful pause, or terrible tragedy. It's up to you to notice these cues. Raise your consciousness and vibration to see what matters. You and I were born into this body for a reason. Life is about growth, transformation, and consciousness. But we don't always see it from this perspective. Oftentimes, it takes a catalyst for change.

What Really Matters?

It's important for us to realize what really matters. Don't you agree? Stuff piles up and loses its significance almost immediately. The clothes you *needed*. The toys your child *wanted* clutter your house. Money spent and time wasted. What is your return on investment? Tomorrow isn't promised, yet we act like it is. We worry, rush, or wallow in misery, not realizing the greatness of each new day. The only thing that matters is your point of view. Ego says, "I'm tired of fighting, hurting, and being alone. I can't take it anymore. I give up." Spirit says, "You are loved, you have purpose and so much potential." The angel is on one side and the devil is on the other. It's a battle between good and evil. You must navigate this duality and decide which voice you will listen to. Don't allow the egoic voice of need or greed to limit your life. Learn how to overcome the social conditioning that depletes loving relationships.

The years Dad was absent from my life because of my interracial relationship didn't mean he didn't care about me or love me. He didn't know how to deal with the situation because of his own screen that was clouded by prejudice and conditioning from his upbringing. We lost precious time together because of the egoic influence, but thankfully we were able to make up lost time later with Caysen by our side. Sometimes, what we need is a different perspective to see. Follow the path of least resistance—it's usually led by love.

Perseverance, pain, and pleasure... it's all a part of the game of LIFE. It's the simple things that matter. Time. Memories. The air you breathe. Your heartbeat. Oxygen. Think about all we take for granted. For example, trees give our planet life and allow us to breathe every second of every day. Yet, we cut these life-giving gifts down to produce garbage. Half of our planet is just operating to make more garbage. Our minds are ruled by corruption and distracted by shiny things. We are losing sight of what truly matters! The only time we can make a change is now. Any transformation must begin with you and your awareness. So, change how you view each day. Decide what matters for you. For your family. For your future.

Life happens between the rise and fall of prejudice, politics, and projections. Between the hopes, dreams, and perceived failures. Between the relationships, resentment, and reflections. Life happens between the rise and fall of it all. Between a family grieving the loss of a loved one and the blessing of a newborn child. Between every prayer, celebration, and separation. Between a failed marriage and the broken family torn in between. Life continues between every breath, thought, and emotion expressed. It's a beautiful symphony of energy exchange that is recorded *behind the screen* and stored in your subconscious memory bank. It becomes your program and drives your body throughout your *Life Timeline*. Life is a journey of learning, unlearning, feeling, and expressing. It's a **journey of consciousness.**

"Love is what we are born with. Fear is what we learn. The spiritual journey is the unlearning of fear and prejudices and the acceptance of love back in our hearts. Love is the essential reality and our purpose on earth. To be consciously aware of it, to experience love in ourselves and others, is the meaning of life. Meaning does not lie in things. Meaning lies in us." [71]
—Marianne Williamson

Exercise: What Really Matters?

Are you caught up in a program or way of thinking that is inhibiting your transformation? Ask yourself these questions about what really matters in your life. Write your reflection in the *Life Timeline Journal*.

- ~ What makes *today* matter? Why?
- ~ Where do you spend the majority of your time and attention? Why does that matter?
- ~ What will matter tomorrow? A year from now? Five years from now?
- ~ What do you think matters when you take your last breath of air?
    - ~ Is it that Michael Kors purse you wanted?
    - ~ How well your hair looks or if your nails are done?
    - ~ The designer clothes in your closet?
    - ~ The type of car you drive?
    - ~ The number of Facebook friends you have?
- ~ What really matters? Are you giving that your time and attention?

~ If not, what should you do differently? Make a list of what truly matters. You can use this list to help with Step 6—Reprogram.

Chapter 13
Reprogram and Resonate

Creating a New Story

"The Law of Attraction states that whatever you focus on, think about, read about, and talk about intensely, you're going to attract more of into your life." [72]
—Jack Canfield

Congratulations, you have come a long way! I hope this has been a valuable journey so far, as you have reflected on your *Life Timeline* while peeking *behind the screen* of my mine. As you notice your own mental conditioning, apply Steps 1 – 5 to overcome the subconscious program, and see life from a new perspective. I know it's not easy to go back into your past and recall negative memories and experiences, but to reach a point where you can release it all, reprogram your mind, and resonate in the energy of living a life you love, you must do the work. You can have the peace, freedom, love, and happiness you deserve. Just by being aware the layers of conditioning exist, you reduce their power over you. Continue through the steps, repeat as needed, practice each with clear intention, take action daily, and hold on to the belief that your transformation is taking root.

Just as any seed needs good soil to grow, your mind needs a functional program to initiate the right responses. If you have over a decade of conditioning to undo, then this process will take time. Focus your time and energy on this system, be consistent, and do not give up. Most people give up just before they reach their breakthrough. Don't be like most people. You are just getting to the fun part!

We are about to embark on the last two steps of the 7-Step system: Reprogram and Resonate. You will create a new program for your subconscious mind to follow. The best part, you get to condition yourself the way you want to think and feel. These steps guide you in reprogramming a new, productive way of thinking to allow your dreams to start taking root. You will create the blueprints for a life you intend to co-create. When you do, the Universe will begin working with you. The law of attraction and the law of resonance will be activated. As you increase your awareness and begin living life in peace and happiness, opportunities will come out of nowhere. The ever-expanding and infinite universe is always providing. It's when you shift your vibrational frequency and energy to a higher realm that you attract what's been seeking you all along. Your mind, body, and soul will be balanced. Get ready to manifest miracles.

Step 6 – REPROGRAM:

After isolating the old program and releasing the energy from your past, you are ready to create a new story by reprogramming your mind. You are the artist of your new reality. You have the opportunity to define the details of a life that brings you complete joy. It's a freeing process to walk in your truth, understand your purpose, ignite your passion, and practice gratitude. This step challenges you to decide what really matters. Reflect on your notes from the exercise in Chapter 12. Incorporate your findings in this step. Consider a future that brings a smile to your face and a sense of purpose to your soul. Most people spend more time planning for a vacation than consciously planning their future. Focus your time and attention on manifesting a life of your dreams and the vacations will follow. The frequency of any channel you're tuned to becomes your programmed way of life. Sometimes you need to change the channel, and tune into a new frequency of being. Draft a new story into your mind. Initiate this story with a burning desire for something greater that allows you to serve a bigger purpose. When your heart and mind are aligned with positive thoughts and feelings, you literally become a tuning fork in the Universe, broadcasting that signal. This is precisely how you will attract opportunities to manifest your dreams. Gandhi said:

> *Your beliefs become your thoughts,*
> *Your thoughts become your words,*
> *Your words become your actions,*
> *Your actions become your habits,*
> *Your habits become your values,*
> *Your values become your destiny.*[73]

Author and educator Kendra Cherry, in an online article titled "How Experience Changes Brain Plasticity," explains the amazing ability of the brain to heal:

> *Early researchers believed that neurogenesis, or the creation of new neurons, stopped shortly after birth. Today, it's understood that the brain possesses the remarkable capacity to reorganize pathways, create new connections, and, in some cases, even create new neurons—a concept called neuroplasticity, or brain plasticity.*[74]

Science proves that our brains can be reprogrammed at any time throughout our life. We can rewire and fire new synaptic connections, overwriting the old program. This means you can overcome addictions, bad habits, unconscious behavior patterns, depression, anxiety, and many other issues that may not be serving your growth and transformation.

REPROGRAM AND RESONATE

Begin to see through your cleansed, unbiased screen into your future. See your future self; transformed and living a life beyond your wildest dreams. See that everything you wanted has come to fruition. You are happy, expressing love and gratitude, thereby attracting many abundant opportunities. What are those opportunities? Maybe you are at the pinnacle of your career, or you started your own business successfully. Maybe you met the love of your life and the two of you are traveling the world. Maybe you have overcome an addiction and found your true calling. Whatever your story is, I invite you to dream it up with no limitations. Imagination is the key to success. You must create this picture in your mind's eye first. The currency of the Universe is ideas, not money! You are working with limitless power, so anything is possible. Remember that everything happens twice, first in thought, then in form. Let your imagination run wild and envision this life in vivid detail. Clarity is power. You can take control of the "regularly scheduled program" and interrupt the broadcast, if you will.

Reprogramming is like being born again or installing new computer software. This time, you have the power to choose what is installed. The key here is to forgo the need to know how you will bridge the gap between your life now and the one you are dreaming up in your mind. Do not allow the ego to deter you with the fear, doubt, or worry of how you can make this dream come true. Leave the *how* up to the Source of creation who unites all possibilities at once. We aren't capable of reading the energetic barometer of all things in the Universe, but the almighty Creator is. The only limitation is **your own mind.**

Repeat the following out loud:

"I have a power breathing me that is greater than any condition or circumstance, and I am worthy of having my dreams come true.
I AM, that which I say I AM.
I CAN have this life,
I WILL have this life,
I AM living this life with purpose and passion.
I'm so happy and grateful for..."
(Now explain your life in vivid detail, the way you would LOVE to live it)
And GO!

Vision it... Write it... Speak it out loud... every day. This is your dream. "You can't get TO your dream. You must come FROM it,"[75] as my mentor, Mary Morrissey, always said. You must get crystal clear about every detail of the life you want to create, so you can wire new neuro-circuitry into your brain. Just like a builder needs a blueprint for a building, you need a blueprint for the future life you intend to manifest. Having this blueprint will guide your thoughts and feelings to create new synaptic connections in your brain. The more you envision that future in your mind—sensing, feeling, tasting, hearing, and smelling it as if you are living that life right now—the more you train your mind. This activates your Reticular Activating System (RAS) to bring into your awareness anything that matches those cues. This network of neurons, located in the brain stem, is your filter through navigating all the millions of sensational inputs every day. It filters into your awareness anything you are paying attention to or thinking about and filters out all the extra stuff you aren't focusing on.

Let's put this in context a bit. Have you ever bought a new car—and then noticed that car everywhere? They didn't just manufacture a bunch of those cars and sell them off in your region. No. This is your Reticular Activating System at work. Because you have a new car, you are aware of this car. With that awareness, your RAS shows you the car while you drive through thousands of cars in traffic. It's your awareness filter. If you train your brain to begin looking for opportunities in your outside environment based on these inputs, you will see opportunities you otherwise wouldn't have seen because your RAS wasn't looking for them. You are staging the future with what you want. Don't forget, you have a supercomputer sitting right between your ears and behind your eyes, connecting all the circuitry controlling your body—and it's free to use. You just need to guide it with your descriptive visualization to form new neural pathways that will become your new way of thinking. A new program, one you consciously create. See your new life on your screen now, so that later you can actually live it. Your subconscious mind cannot tell the difference between a vision or reality. That's why many people use visualization as a tool for manifestation—they understand how the subconscious mind works. It's guided by the pictures it sees **on your screen.**

> "You must learn a new way to think before you can master a new way to be." [76]
> —Marianne Williamson

Begin every vision with expansive energy (happiness) and grateful expectation. Carry that burning desire and grateful expectation into your day, every day. Just like athletes train their bodies, you must train your mind to achieve this vision or dream. Practicing gratitude raises your vibrational frequency. It's one of the strongest emotions and it can shift your energy in the moment. Ultimately, you can reprogram your brain to fire and wire thoughts full of gratitude unconsciously. This takes time, practice, and dedication, but when you make it a part of your daily routine, it will become a habit. Be intentional with habits you want to create. Notice the habits you need to override.

Speak your visualization out loud. This gives life to your words. Always begin your sentence with, "I am so happy and grateful...." The Law of Attraction is a real universal law that says you can attract anything by having a "burning desire and grateful expectation." This combo tells the Universe what you want and that you are ready to receive it, because you believe in it. This is key—you must believe you can have it. Here is an example of my dream / visualization for my future life:

> I am so happy and grateful that I'm able to provide for Caysen physically, mentally, spiritually, financially, and emotionally, so he grows up with a sense of security, love, compassion, and gratitude in his heart. I am so happy and grateful my mom has been a part of our lives and continues to teach Caysen the wonders of the world. Caysen has grown up to be a compassionate, caring, smart, and successful young man.
>
> I am so happy and grateful that I met the man of my dreams. His smile ignites my senses, and his kiss sets my soul on fire. The electricity I receive through every kiss excites every electron in my energy being. We have the best love. I AM SO HAPPY AND GRATEFUL FOR the touch of his beautiful hand running down my spine. The

tender kiss he gives me every morning with a bright, big, good morning smile. The way he interacts with Caysen and empowers him to reap the benefits of hard work. Together, they make my soul sing. Seeing them laugh, talk, and grow together makes every second of my life worthwhile. He is my soulmate and best friend, who reminds me of his love and appreciation through simple gestures, like sending me the most beautiful flowers in the most unexpected times.

We live in a beautiful house with many windows overlooking the ocean. Our family continues to grow, and we enjoy so much quality time together. We are all healthy, extremely happy, and successful.

My book, "Behind the Screen," is an international best seller. Oprah has interviewed me, and my schedule is booked solid for the next two years with conferences, workshops, and keynote speaking engagements all over the world. I have a team of people employed by Infinite Soulutions, LLC, and our coaching programs are sold out. Caysen is introducing me on stage and leading Vision Workshops with Youth Groups. We have been able to reach, teach, and transform hundreds of thousands of people's lives and we continue to work on teaching the Laws of the Universe to the masses, so they understand the power they hold.... This or something **even greater still.**

And that is how it's done! When you finish your dream, say out loud, "This or something even greater still!" Hold your dream with an open mind and grateful heart, because the Universe is infinitely abundant, and you may attract something even greater still. All right, my friend, it's your turn.

Exercise: Step 6 – Create a Vision

Close your eyes. Take a deep breath. Imagine you are walking into the life of your dreams at least three years from now. Enter into a future with limitless potential. There is nothing holding you back—no limitations, conditions, or fear. Begin by saying, "I am so happy and grateful...." Then envision yourself living your best life. Don't even think about how this will happen. Just see your dream with childlike imagination. See it, smell it, five-sense it in your mind, body, and soul.

Once you have visualized it, you need to write that vision down in explicit detail. Do so now in your *Life Timeline Journal*.

Next, speak your vision out loud. Your breath will give life to the words. The vibration of your voice fuels the words to flow into the Universe that manifests all existence. The feeling tone of your energy being will tune into the frequency of that channel. Continue this daily.

Believe that you can co-create this life, because you can, 100 percent! The only thing that will block you from attracting this is your own fear, doubt, or worry. The egoic lens shadows your potential. Delete it from the story. Believe fully in your dream with your whole mind, body, and soul. Let the Universe do the work with you.

Mythologist Joseph Campbell said, "What each must seek in his life never was on land or sea. It is something out of his own unique potentiality for experience, something that never has been and never could have been experienced by anyone else."[77]

Always focus your attention on what you want, not what you don't want. That is where your energy will flow. Your brain filters inputs, so if you say, "I don't want to be sick," it's focusing on the mere thought of being sick—unconsciously attracting that type of energy. Focus on what you want in your health, relationships, at school, or in your career. Allow your Reticular Activating System to focus on what you want to manifest through its powerful lens while evaluating everything in your external environment. The screen inside your mind will become your reality outside, so be mindful of your thoughts and intentions. Be conscious of the power you hold. Make this a part of your daily practice. *Notice what you are noticing.* Your belief that all things are lining up in perfect order for the future you want will allow the Universe to start working in your favor.

Reprogram and Resonate (Step 6 and 7) must be done simultaneously. You attract the vision of your new story and way of thinking by resonating with the feeling tone of it.

This leads us to the last step, **Step 7 – Resonate.**

Step 7 – RESONATE:

Establish a feeling tone in your body now. You become a vibrational match for the person living your dream by resonating in that energy. Remember how you look in your dream. What are you doing? Where, why, when, and with whom do you spend your time? What makes your soul come alive in the dream? Weave that dream into the fabric of your life. Wear it. Feel the energy of every emotion while you imagine living that joyous life right now. Feel the energy of this dream in your body from now on. Each time you think about or speak about your new story (your fulfilling life), you feel like you are living this way currently. Your subconscious mind doesn't know the difference. Through your resonance, your energetic amplification will match the vibrational frequency of what you are trying to attract. Recall the notion mentioned earlier about becoming a tuning fork. The signal you broadcast is interpreted by the Universe and matched up with similar frequencies. It's all energy—waves of possibility within the electromagnetic spectrum. Your quality of consciousness allows you to tune into a particular frequency through your level of vibration. Like changing the channel on your radio dial, if you tune to 103.9 FM, you will not get 95.1 FM. Those are two different channels. Tune your thoughts, feelings and beliefs to the channel or state of being you want. In doing so, you attract that into your reality.

If you are seeking happiness, you must BE HAPPY now. Think happy, feel happy, act happy—as if you are that person now. Your energetic vibrational frequency must resonate at the level that matches that of happiness. Frequency is measured by hertz—a measurement equal to one event per second.[78] According to over 20 years of research done by Dr. David R. Hawkins, who first introduced the Map of Consciousness® in his book, *Power vs. Force*, he created a map on the scales of human consciousness using a logarithmic scale of 1 to 1,000. Shame, guilt, and apathy have the lowest energetic frequency, whereas peace and enlightenment are at the top of the scale. The vibrational frequency of joy is 540.[79] In summary, the work of Dr. Hawkins proves to us that your level of consciousness emits an energetic frequency that can be measured. The infinitely expanding Universe has natural laws that decipher your energetic frequency and match you with similar sources of energy.

REPROGRAM AND RESONATE

I have to assume the energy of being an International Best-Selling Author and sold out speaker now. In doing so, I become a vibrational match to attract opportunities within this landscape to me. That makes me feel excited and grateful to see my hard work is paying off. I feel like a shining star because Oprah Winfrey interviewed me. I cannot stop smiling. I go to bed every night with a heart full of gratitude and wake up energized to begin my day. I get to influence young people and empower them to see through a clear screen. I feel enlightened, like I'm walking on a cloud. My energy body feels light and aligned with my purpose for being.

It's so beautiful when you can see clearly. This is not hocus-pocus, "woo-woo" stuff. The Law of Gravity may be invisible, but it's real—what goes up must come down. The Laws of Vibration and Resonance are also invisible, but very much real. In fact, these Universal Laws have been studied by transformational masters like Raymond Hollywell, who wrote the book, *Working with the Law*, which explains eleven Universal Laws of life, success, and happiness. The book was written in 1939 and is taught in workshops around the world. In fact, I've taught several of these workshops and offer a 12-week Coaching Program for Working with the Law. Additionally, Andrew Carnegie, leader of the American steel industry in the nineteenth century, became one of the richest men in the world. Throughout his life, he learned these principles and wanted to share this knowledge with the masses. He did this by mentoring Author Napoleon Hill, offering him a twenty-year assignment. Carnegie introduced Hill to 100 of the richest men at that time, including Alexander Graham Bell, Thomas Edison, and Henry Ford. The idea was for Hill to study these successful people, and to distill their wisdom into easy-to-digest secrets that could be shared with the public. He did this in the infamous book *Think and Grow Rich*. Tony Robbins, Mary Morrissey, Michael Beckwith, and many other way-showers continue to transform people's lives by sharing these truths. These Universal Laws exist and you can learn to harness them for your own success and happiness. They are aligned with the laws of nature and our planetary function.

Our world is a living, breathing, pulsing organism. Every action creates a reaction. Every feeling gives off a vibration at a certain frequency, and resonance determines what will be manifested or brought into your physical reality. Quantum Physics proves that when you uncover what's beneath the surface microscopically, every physical object in our world is simply a vibrating subatomic particle of energy. In other words, everything is energy, vibrating at certain levels or frequencies. When you radiate that vibration as if you are living your dream now, you are signaling to the Universe (like dropping a pin on a map) your availability and intention to manifest that vision into reality. It says, "Universe, here I am, I am ready to be matched with this exact same frequency!" And so it is….

Remember Step 3 – Feel It? You had to feel the emotions from the past so you could bring them to the surface for release. Now, Step 7 is about feeling those emotions of living your dream life now. Commit to this system of transformation for at least ninety days. Focus all your conscious attention on your new life and your new way of thinking, feeling, and acting. Commit to feeling like the person who is living your dream life and take action steps each day to begin firing and wiring new neurological connections in your brain. Wake up each day with grateful expectation and a burning desire to manifest this new life. It fills you with so much peace, joy, and excitement that you can't help but talk about it. Think about it, feel it, dream about it, speak it out loud, every day. Start resonating in that energy to give your dream life so that you may begin attracting opportunities. Believe in the possibility of abundance and prosperity and then tune yourself to that channel.

Honestly, I had to remove the word "crazy" from my vocabulary, because once you begin to do this work consciously, crazy things happen. Are they miracles? Maybe. Is it luck? Perhaps. Or is it just the work of the great I AM? I believe in I AM! Once you experience this firsthand and repeatedly, in my opinion, it validates the system of transformation. I have vetted and verified this system many times in the past ten years, so believe me, this stuff works. It can work for you, too.

You are what you think and say because your subconscious mind interprets it this way. How you feel is what you attract. You react to what you attract, causing a result that becomes your experience and shapes your reality. Make it positive. Avoid feeling angry, stressed, or fearful. These are low vibrational frequencies of emotion viewed through the egoic screen that will only inhibit your ability to manifest anything different. Believe in a higher power. You are resetting your state of being through this system of transformation. Reset with a purpose. Your level of consciousness at any given moment is power. Peace and enlightenment should be the goal. Raising human consciousness is mine.

Exercise: Step 7 – Become the New You

Describe your state of being in the *Life Timeline Journal*. As you envision yourself living this new way of life, how do you feel? What makes you feel this way? Be descriptive with every feeling or emotion that comes up, so you can assume that feeling tone right away. Decide what you can do today to feel this way?

What can you do tomorrow and the next day? Do it. Take action. Be creative and get excited about this process. It's fun… and it works.

Chapter 14
Stepping into Your Truth

Accountability is Key

> "Every intention sets energy into motion, whether you are aware of it or not." [80]
> —Gary Zukav

After you have successfully completed Steps 1 – 7, you will rinse your mind, body, and soul with love and gratitude. Just as you wash your clothes and hang them out to dry on a clothesline, you need to rinse your mental capacities and allow them time to reset with clarity. Refresh and reset each day with your burning desire and grateful expectation. It takes time to reprogram a conditioned way of living, thinking, feeling, and acting. That's why you rinse and repeat.

This must become your new way of living. Accountability is key. Do you hold yourself accountable to brush your teeth every day and wash your clothes when they get dirty? The same must hold true for your way of thinking and feeling. Most people need a support system or accountability partner to keep them on track. If you are like most, you should consider the 12-week coaching program to enhance your progress. This system of transformation is most effective when you have a dedicated coach and a community of people to connect with. That's why Infinite SOULutions, LLC offers a 12-week coaching program to guide you through rinsing and repeating Steps 1 – 7 of the *Life Timeline System of Transformation*, so you can overcome your subconscious programming, master your mindset, and co-create a life that you deserve. **Go to www.carrie-schmidt.com to learn more and/or to schedule a complimentary strategy session using CODE: BEHINDTHESCREEN.**

Remember, the *Life Timeline* is a tool to help you analyze your thought processes, emotional state of being, decisions, actions/reactions, and the results you have accumulated from the day you were born to this very moment in time. Use it to become more conscious and map out the experiences of your life, whether they are positive or negative. Notate the ages you first experienced a certain way of thinking and feeling on your *Life Timeline*. Narrow your focus and look for commonalities or repeating patterns that may keep showing up in different relationships or circumstances over time. Notice the patterns and identify their inception point without giving them your power. Flip your perspective to that of a conscious observer who can objectively identify what the Universe may have been trying to show you. Open your mind up to new possibilities.

As you pin up memories and experiences on your *Life Timeline* the way you would hang clothes on a clothesline, release the hurtful experiences from your energy body. Allow the Universe to recycle them. With a fresh, clean screen, you can start taking control at the wheel of your life. Then the bonds of the past no longer have control over your mind and body and you are free to imagine a new way of living. You realize that the ego is an invisible force to which you have been giving power. Raise your consciousness and win the game. Your spiritual power is stronger than the ego's influence. The only condition or limitation exists in your own mind through your belief. Believe in something greater. Dream up the life you want to live, now. This moment is all you have.

Through your divine connection, your consciousness gives you power. Create the blueprint of your dream life in your mind now, then resonate with its soul-fulfilling energy. Align your mind and body to radiate the frequency of joy, balance, and prosperity. Train your mind to look for the opportunities and believe in the manifestation of miracles. Your Reticular Activating System does the work for you. Look at your glass and see it overflowing—there is no room for emptiness. Your cup is connected to divine fluidity. See your dream come to fruition. Continue rinsing and repeating until a new program takes root in your subconscious mind.

Act as if you are already living that dream and continue to practice gratitude for all that you are manifesting. You can begin by taking baby steps. The Universe evolves based upon your belief. Believe in your power and greatness. Believe that you are capable and worthy to have this life. Open your mind, heart, and soul to a way of being—free, loved, and fulfilled. When your old programming kicks in—become aware of it. Stop it! Tag it and remember it for what it is; an unconscious automatic response you developed to survive your past. It doesn't have power over you anymore because you have released that energy, which empowers you to see the faulty program through a cleaner screen. Notice when it comes up for you. Pause without engaging emotion and breathe. Focus on the clean air filling your lungs with life and remember your new program or dream. Focus on the new story you are co-creating within the infinitely expanding, loving universe. Watch your new, soul-serving story play across your screen. Pause and allow the present moment to override your old way of being. Each time you do this, you train your mind and body. You prove that you are in control, not your ego or your unconscious mind. Let them know who is running the show. **I AM!**

Positive Affirmations

Affirmations are a powerful tool to reprogram your subconscious mind. Look up positive affirmations on YouTube and listen to them. Create a playlist of your favorite affirmations. You can listen to them while you sleep at night, because your subconscious mind never sleeps. It listens and records. You can write positive affirmations as well and read them each day. What you pay attention to will increase, so why not focus on everything you want to manifest? Use the tools at your disposal to help your mind evolve faster.

Your mind powers your body, unconsciously, so use your mind to fuel your body with good energy. You have the spirit of God inside you all the time, and it's through your awareness in every present moment that you can activate its power. Rinse old programs with a golden light of love and hang them up on your *Life Timeline*. Repeat the process so your brain can fire and wire new synaptic connections, forging a healthier way of thinking. Your new way of thinking will take root and, with repetition, will override the faulty program that hasn't been serving you. New thoughts, sourced through positive inputs, create healthier feeling tones. You vibrate higher, allowing the cells in your body to function freely. Stop beating yourself up. Your negative self-talk or outward judgment only restricts your energy body. It makes you shrink like an old grape. Speak in a way that is positive and uplifting. Take back your power. Read, write, or watch inspirational movies and documentaries. Connect with people who are doing the same. Surround yourself with a community of believers and achievers. Make a commitment to transform your life in a positive, influential way. Dedication, consistency, and faith will provide the fruits of your labor. Don't wait until it is too late.

The Wake-Up Call
It's unfortunate that for many people, death, tragedy, or disease provide a wake-up call in their lives. A powerful force disrupts

their regularly scheduled program. It forces them to wake up and see life from a brand new perspective.

Life is short. Your whole world could change drastically, in an instant. Tomorrow is not promised to anyone. I realized this on Father's Day 2013 when my father had to be Life Flighted to the ICU in a Pittsburgh hospital. It scared Dad to fly, and he swore he would never fly in an airplane, no matter what. That day, he had no choice. Doctors had admitted him to our local hometown hospital the day before for pneumonia and he was having a hard time breathing. Caysen and I went to visit, along with my sister, Kim and brother-in-law, Jim. The doctors had hooked him up to many monitors and he was getting continuous breathing treatments. We spent a few hours visiting, reminiscing, and joking around like we always did. We didn't realize, at that time, his condition would not improve. I wish I had known that would be the last time my son would see his Papa; the only male figure in his life.

The following day, Caysen and I had gone out to get a Father's Day balloon and card to take to the hospital when I got a call—Dad had taken a turn for the worse. This hospital could not treat his worsening condition. Kim, Jim, and I rushed to the hospital and were asked to decide immediately which hospital to Life Flight him to: Pittsburgh or Cleveland. I sat on the cold hospital floor, my head between my knees, fighting back the tears pouring down my face. Jim knelt beside me and rubbed my back, trying to console me. There was nothing we could do. Off we went into the parking lot, where I watched Dad's stretcher wheeled to the helicopter. That was his first flight.

We drove straight to Pittsburgh, a little over an hour's drive. Upon our arrival at the hospital ICU, they wouldn't let us in to see him or even give us an update—they were working to keep him alive. This was how he spent his last Father's Day—it's a day I will never forget. I didn't believe he was going to die. They got him stabilized, and he was hospitalized for about a week. I drove back and forth each day to the hospital to be by his side, trying to give him positive energy to fight through his condition. He was unconscious, unable to talk. His kidneys were shutting down and his lungs were not functioning. It wasn't looking good. I hated to leave him, but I had to go back to work.

The next day, I got a call from the nurses at work. Dad had to be put on life support. They needed Kim and me to come to the hospital to make decisions for him. My Dad had never written a will or assigned anyone as Power of Attorney in the event he could not decide for himself. This was that time. The burden of this decision was placed on my sister and me. Did we keep him on life support and pray for recovery, even though he'd need dialysis for the rest of his life? He had just turned sixty! Kim and I had different opinions. I believed in God and that miracles can happen. She never had much faith or a belief in a higher power. She thought Dad would not want to be on life support. It was the worst day.

Sitting in that room with Kim, going over the "what-if's" and the "what-would-Dad-want-to-do's?" I had a giant hole in my stomach. I felt like I was dreaming. This couldn't be happening. My Dad and Caysen should have more time together. Dad could watch Caysen play football and be his number one fan. He'd see him graduate high school and give him fatherly advice. There was still time left to live. Time with loved ones, this priceless gift we so often take for granted is not promised to any of us.

My sister convinced me that Dad would not want to be on life support. So, I agreed with her, and we let the nurses take him off the machine that was keeping his blood pumping with oxygen since his lungs had shut down. I said my goodbyes and kissed Dad's forehead, then sat on the floor at the edge of his bed while my sister did the same. My sister sat on his bedside, holding his hand while the nurse turned off the machine. Once again, I was sitting on the cold hospital floor sobbing, head between my knees, tears streaming down my face. I could not bear to see him lifeless. I never looked at him again; I didn't want to relive that memory. It only took a few minutes until we heard the flat line beep. He had passed away. I couldn't describe that feeling to you in words. It was devastating. I would never see my father again. As we walked out of that hospital, I felt like death. Even worse, I had to break the news to my six-year-old son. "Papa's gone." That was awful. The hardest day of my life. Caysen was only six years old and heartbroken. It's terrible to lose a parent, or any loved one for that matter. It gave me a different perspective on life.

Dad's death was the second turning point or wake-up call in my life (the first being Caysen's birth). The unexpected loss of my father cleaned my screen once again. It forced me to focus on what really mattered. My loved ones. My time. My purpose. You don't know how much time you have, so taking action on your aspirations is critical. Spending quality time with loved ones and being present for each moment is profoundly important. We all need to be reminded of this now and again. Be present and aware of the gift of life. My consciousness expanded as a result of this life-changing loss. I learned to appreciate every moment and truly feel the joy of seeing my son smile, hearing his deep belly laugh, and watching him learn new things. I decided that from here on out, I would live my life with clear intention and let nothing stand in my way of having true peace and happiness. If I didn't like my life, I knew only I could change it. If I complained about my job, it was time to find one that brought me happiness. If I wasn't happy in a relationship, I ended it. Whatever my soul was yearning for, I went after that passion. Life is too short. Memories matter, not things. I decided my environment would not dictate my happiness. Nothing and no one would stand in the way of my spiritual calling. Don't lose sight of the power you hold. The power that nature provides. Your ability to breathe, walk, talk, decide, connect and love, every second of every day. Become conscious of this gift. Stop focusing on the stuff that doesn't matter. You are staring death in the face. Your outfit, how your hair looks, what a stranger thinks about you, your title, the type of car you drive, how much money you make, or that unopened Snapchat—none of it matters. Everything in this *Life Timeline* depends upon your perspective in every present moment. My perspective shifted. Life is too short to be stuck behind a veil of discontentment or a curtain of fear.

    I wised up, rose up, and took action. My whole life, I had wanted to move south. Every day, I had wanted to wake up to sunshine and blue skies. I didn't want to hibernate for six months or half of my life (whichever way you want to see it through the screen). I made it a mission to move from Pennsylvania (where we had less than forty days of sunshine per year) to the Carolinas, Florida, Texas, or Georgia. I didn't care where, I wanted warmer weather, blue skies, and a great school district for my son.

    With that, I set out on a yearlong journey to make my dream a reality. I applied for hundreds of jobs, went on a few interviews, and did a tremendous amount of research. I repeated my saying every day, "I CAN—I WILL—I AM!" "I can move to the south, I will move to the south, I am living in the south!" CCL Container (the company I was working for) agreed to relocate me to Charlotte, NC, to keep me with the company. I had contributed so much that when the CEO and Board of Directors got wind of my impending departure from the company, they set me up with an excellent relocation deal. Mom, Caysen, and I moved to Tega Cay, South Carolina in 2015.

The funny thing is, I believe the stars were aligned and this move was meant to be. Everything fell into perfect order. I ended up meeting my new best friend, Vicki, when I was in South Carolina looking at houses. (Coincidentally, if you recall, one of my imaginary friends was named Vicki). I'd just made an offer on the house I was hoping to buy in South Carolina when I stopped at a local tavern to have lunch and a glass of wine. Vicki was the bartender. I shared my dream and my story with her, and we hit it off, talking and sharing our stories. Vicki had just started this new job after being a stay-at-home Mom for three years. While talking, I got a call from my realtor in Pennsylvania, who informed me I'd received a full-price offer on my house. Within an hour, I got another call that my offer on the SC house was accepted. Vicki and I were both amazed and agreed the stars must be in alignment. I celebrated over a few glasses of wine, then signed the paperwork on both houses that evening in my hotel room. That doesn't happen often! The Universe was working with me because I had a burning desire and grateful expectation, and I took action to manifest my dream into reality.

Two months later, a moving company packed up my house and drove the fifty-three-foot tractor trailer to our new home in Tega Cay, SC. We started a brand-new life in a new town, knowing no one (except my new best friend, Vicki). A fresh start! My dream became a reality. I learned how to become a Master of Manifestation. Caysen, Mom, and I made new friends (some have become our family), and we love living in the Carolinas. Whether it is attending country concerts, visiting breweries, going to baseball and football games, or hanging by the pool on the weekends, life is good! Everything I set my mind to and acted upon turned into reality. Opportunities continued to find me as I focused on manifesting what I wanted for the future. Every year since then, every single one of my dreams has manifested in physical form.

Exercise: Take Action

Reflect on the following questions in your *Life Timeline Journal.*

- ~ How do you relate to this story? Have you ever had a wake-up call that interrupted your scheduled program? What was the catalyst that forced you to see clearly?
- ~ How can you reflect on that "life lesson" and gain a greater understanding of yourself and what your soul may seek? If fear, doubt, or worry were not present in your mind's eye, what would you choose to do differently?
- ~ Make a list of at least three action steps that you will take to initiate your transformation.
- ~ Make sure to assign a due date for each action item.
- ~ When you complete one action, go back to your journal and check off that goal as being completed. Celebrate your ability to follow through on your goals.
- ~ Continue taking action.

Don't wait until it's too late. Don't allow those invisible egoic forces to hold you back from activating your true calling. I encourage you to always *"Live your dream and wear your*

passion." This is my daily goal. I found this quote in the last line of the Holstee Manifesto, the Holstee Company's definition of success, which goes like this...

> "This is your life. Do what you want and do it often.
> If you don't like something, change it.
> If you don't like your job, quit.
> If you don't have enough time, stop watching TV.
> If you are looking for the love of your life, stop; they will be waiting for you when you start doing things you love.
> Stop over-analyzing, life is simple.
> All emotions are beautiful.
> When you eat, appreciate every last bite.
> Life is simple.
> Open your heart, mind and arms to new things and people.
> We are united in our differences.
> Ask the next person you see what their passion is and share your inspiring dream with them.
> Travel often; getting lost will help you find yourself.
> Some opportunities only come once, seize them.
> Life is about the people you meet and the things you create with them, so go out and start creating.
> Life is short, **live your dream and wear your passion**." [81]
> —Holstee Manifesto

Chapter 15
A Roadmap to Fulfilling Your Soul's Purpose

Ask, Act, and You Shall Receive

> *"Ask for what you want and be prepared to get it."* [82]
> —Maya Angelou

Our souls have a purpose. While we may not know what it is or how to find it, we can get curious and conscious about this fact. Repeat the following words out loud:

> *I am more than my body and greater than my mind.*
> *I have a purpose to fulfill in my Life Timeline.*
> *My soul speaks through my passion.*
> *My passion lights me up and makes me feel alive.*

Our soul is always seeking a freer, fuller, and more expansive way to express itself. It speaks to you through your intuition and guides us like nature. We are meant to grow. Evolve. Seek the light. The only conditions limiting our infinite potential are the physical body, egoic mind, and the finite worldly view. Oftentimes, we look at life through a dirty screen. We become conditioned. The relationship, experience, or memory... it carries energy into the present. That's human nature; the nature of Beauty and the Beast. Which side do you see? The visible or invisible; opportunity or limitation; love or fear? It all boils down to your perspective—your state of consciousness at any given second.

Are you stuck? Hungry for more? Tired of getting the same results? Become aware of your old program and the matrix of perception, then take the first action step to shift your life. Join a community of people who are awake and ready for more. Connect to your power to be more. Live more. Allow transformation to consume you from the inside out. We need to wake up for our planet. Let's reveal the truth and consciously join forces to make this world a better place. Stop overconsumption, deforestation, pollution, and industrial development. Stop bullying, fighting, and obsessing over things that do not matter. Let's unravel the layers of deceit, expose the egoic lens, and teach a new way of living to the masses.

Need some more inspiration? Watch the movie, *The Secret*, a documentary released in 2006. This influential film includes, "Interviews with self-proclaimed authors, philosophers, scientists, with an in-depth discussion of visualizing your goals. The audience is shown how they can learn and use 'The Secret' in their everyday lives."[83] If you have not seen this movie yet, I highly recommend watching it. If you incorporate what you learn from the movie and this book into your life—you will reap rewards. I watched the movie when I was pregnant with Caysen. It impacted my outlook on life profoundly. As I look back, I realize this movie gave me the insight, courage, and confidence I needed at that time in my life. Ten years later, I watched this movie with Caysen so he could learn "The Secret." In doing so, I picked up a few golden nuggets, applied them to my situation at that time, and within two days manifested selling a house I had for sale. The house had been sitting on the market for nine months with no offer. Voila, I received a full-price offer right after I made a simple mindset shift. Sometimes, that's all it takes.

Your mind is a master house of power—your body follows its direction. Choose a course that fulfills your soul as you walk into each new day. Don't stay stuck in whatever rut you fell into. Apply this logic to your life—your every action and interaction. Focus on your breath when you get stressed. Believe in your ability to gain control of your mind and have a positive impact on those around you. You can do it. Pursue your passion and live on purpose. Life is short.

Forging a new path in life isn't always easy, but it is worthwhile. The roads are not always smooth. I stumbled on many rocks along the way. Caysen, Mom, and I live in South Carolina and enjoy walking outside in flip-flops during wintertime. It was 70 degrees on Christmas this past year. The sun shines almost every day. I look up at the beautiful Carolina blue skies and thank God for allowing me to harvest my crop, which comes with plenty of advantages and juicy fruit. It feels like I climbed a giant mountain, but now, looking down from the top, I am astonished by the magnitude of abundance from the tiniest perspective. Seeds grow roots that turn into magnificent life-giving trees. Subatomic particles are the basic building blocks of the Universe. Thoughts become things. Blessings can be disguised. We are all one. Consciousness is our superpower. I harnessed the will to turn my situation into a blessing. Or did my blessing become my story?

My blessing was my situation, because it allowed me to grow and find my higher self. I set goals. I said affirmations. I believed that I could achieve everything I thought I could. I was coming from the vision of my dream fulfilled, and year after year, it manifested into perfect form with extra, unexpected enhancements. I got to visit Europe, tour castles in Germany, and ride the bullet train to France. I love to travel, so having the opportunity to travel all over the USA, Mexico, and Canada for work trips was a bonus. My soul challenged me to step out of my comfort zone and pursue my dream of being a consultant. I ventured to Los Angeles and studied with Mary Morrissey to become a Certified Life Mastery Consultant. I started my own coaching and consulting business, Infinite SOULutions, LLC. We put the soul in 'soulutions.' Because I know when you connect to the power of your soul, you can solve any problem. The 'soulutions' are infinite. Today, I help my clients master their mindset, overcome limiting beliefs, start or grow their own business, escape exhausting relationships and unfulfilling jobs. I empower them to gain the clarity and confidence they need to transform their results in life. Now, I'm happy and grateful to lead you and others on this transformational journey to get *behind the screen*, clean it, and see a bright, fulfilling future.

It's been one wild ride, but I would not change a thing. Everything along my *life timeline* has happened for a reason. I try to live every day to the fullest and act when I believe the Universe is trying to tell me something. People enter your life for a reason. Pay attention to that. Cultivate meaningful relationships. Take a vacation—or take a break. Breathe. Say a blessing over your food. Eat healthy. Exercise. Make a To Do List. Check things off. Celebrate your accomplishments and life! Life is great. It will be as great as you allow it to be. Allow yourself to give off and attract good vibes. Recall, everything in life depends on your perspective, energy, vibration.

You must start somewhere. I went from being a single mother on welfare to a highly successful Plant Manager. In fact, at thirty-five, I was promoted to VP/General Manager. It is rare for a woman to hold this kind of title in a male-dominated manufacturing industry. I went from selling drugs to reading personal development and self-help books. I changed my mindset from being a victim to being a person with clear intention, resiliency, and a burning desire for excellence. I resonated in the energy of believing and achieving every goal with grateful expectation. I made the changes. No one else around me changed; I did. That positive change brought about countless opportunities that I was open to accepting through my conscious interactions. Every day gets better.

Love is the Way

Be grateful for the power you were born with. It's your awareness of love that allows you to radiate at a higher vibrational frequency. When you are one with your truth and purpose, you feel lighter, more carefree, less stressed, and complete. All truth lies in love. All meaning exists in the essence of unity and oneness. Practice increasing your consciousness and believing in your ability to manifest miracles. Resonate in the energy of your greatness and resolve to evolve. Before you know it, you will replace your old program with one you have created, allowing you to live in peace and happiness.

Your vulnerability is a resource that makes you human. It allows your truth to shine through your soul and that light makes all the difference in the world. When you don't have to hide behind a fake veil, you can open your heart, show your scars, and own your truth. I'm doing that in this book. I'm doing it to show you that you can, too. You are not alone. The fact that you are reading this book makes it likely we have many things in common. For example, maybe your boyfriend cheated on you—so did mine, for nine years. Maybe you end up in terrible relationships that leave you broken—so do countless women. Maybe your childhood wasn't easy. That distress has taken a toll on your energy being. Perhaps you struggle with addiction, anxiety, or depression. There are millions of people out there who suffer *behind the screen*. You could be a single parent struggling to get by—tired of fighting the battle alone. Don't be a Lone Ranger carrying pounds of pain, holding on to resentment from the past.

When attending my first DreamBuilder Live conference in Los Angeles with Mary Morrissey a few years ago, I had a lightning bolt moment. "Release the Lone Ranger Syndrome!" I realized that I'd acquired this syndrome of doing everything alone and not asking for help. I held on to resentment for the mere fact that I had to do it all alone. The truth is, I didn't. I just didn't want to ask for help. I carried the wall around with me. Instead of releasing the anguish, showing my vulnerability, and asking for help, I kept climbing the mountain with 100 pounds on my back. On the way up, I would think to myself, "Fuck everyone else. I can do it myself." This made me more bitter. We are not meant to struggle alone. We are not meant to bottle up our pain and emotions, either. Every battle teaches us what we need to evolve, even the ones we may not understand.

When you build walls to survive suffering, they block you from abundance. They block you from receiving love. Become open to the portal of opportunity to attract your dreams and desires. Harmonize with the flow of unconditional love. Compassion. Peace. Strength. Patience. Prosperity. Join forces with your Source to co-create. Let your guard down. Ask for help. That doesn't make you weak. In fact, it displays your strength and conscious intention to make a positive change. It opens the door for the Universe to deliver what you need.

We can't change the past and you should regret nothing that has happened in your life, because it made you who you are today. Believe me, I know how past trauma can stimulate self-sabotaging habits and self-esteem issues. I haven't always loved myself, and I struggle daily with negative self-talk. I hit the internal pause button when I notice my mind going astray. I pause and breathe into the present moment to regain my awareness. I am what I think, and I attract what I feel. My power is restored as soon as I regain consciousness. I am a good person with good intentions. I love my spirit—the one that isn't engaged with any part of ego. We all serve our egoic mind, because that is human nature. Maybe that is what makes us human. Either way, we are multi-faceted beings equipped with love in our hearts. Most of us live our lives doing the best we can or striving to be better. If not, then there is suffering. Love removes suffering.

Spirituality and religion have guided humans towards love, but there is still evil in the world. We can fall prey to our weaknesses and develop negative habits or unconscious tendencies that weigh us down. The energy of another person or group of people can weigh you down or lift you up. Their screens play a role in their positive or negative vibration. You feel their energy. They feel yours. Choose to harmonize with love and have a greater influence on others around you. When you get the wake-up call and start seeing life from a different perspective, you change. Breaking news interrupts your regular program. You realize the truth. *A Course in Miracles* says, "Perfect love casts out fear, if fear exists, then there is not perfect love."[84]

You are perfect as you are. You don't need someone to complete you. You don't need a designer purse or makeup to enhance your beauty. You are beautiful and complete already. I wish I'd known this when I was fourteen. You were born complete. Lean into this truth. Forgiveness and compassion are key. Humble yourself under God's mighty hand. The ego is after your mind and your dreams. It prowls around like a hungry lion, waiting for the opportunity to feed on your fear. It's like a creepy crawler sneaking into your thoughts and blinding your vision. It makes your screen look thick and shadowy, forcing you to believe the other side of your comfort zone is scary and difficult. The ego and its fake lens fool us all. It tricks us into believing we are alone or unloved. We are brainwashed to believe in perfection and to yearn for riches. We avoid taking chances and going after our dreams because the screen is so full of fear and doubt. Break down the fortress walls you built long ago and let the light of this new day in.

Like trees and plants, we need light. We yearn for its warmth. The sun shines light upon every new day. Love does, too. Allow the power of love and light to shine into your life and illuminate a clear path. We all want to overcome our trials and tribulations and move from the darkness into the light. We all want peace and happiness in our lives. In this way (and so many more), we are one. We are all seeking the truth: Love. You don't have to run or hide anymore, because your truth will set you free. That's why I'm grateful for the hand of God, who turns darkness into light. He has a plan—and you hold his power. You hold the blueprints. So, stop believing in illusions hosted by the ego, and start to notice the screen through which you have been viewing life. If it needs cleaning, begin applying the *7-Step Life Timeline System of Transformation*. Leave fear at the doorstep of your faith. Raise your level of consciousness and vibrational frequency. You will THRIVE when you stop trying to survive with such little belief. To believe is to surrender to a higher power. You can't understand how your life will change. Only the creator does. You co-create with the Universe through your level of consciousness. That energy vibrates at a certain frequency, tuning you into the ether. It's like a radio station in the Universe that you choose. Tune your channel to one that makes your soul sing. Don't wait until it's too late. Tomorrow is not promised. Take action now, because life happens between the rise and fall of it all.

Following is a list of principles and beliefs that provide the foundation for the *Life Timeline System of Transformation*. You should understand and apply each concept to your everyday life from here on out. Share the truth with others who are open to clearing their screens. All transformation begins with one word, one action, one focus—awareness. Once you begin practicing this new way of living you will start to see phenomena or experience unexplainable coincidences. Be sure to pay attention to all the signs and signals. Universal consciousness is at play. Dr. Wayne Dyer often said, "When you change the way you look at things, the things you look at change." [85]

Principles of the Program

Please take a moment to read the underlying principles of the Program.

- ~ Everything in the Universe is made up of energy.
- ~ Everything vibrates at one frequency or another.
- ~ Energy can have a positive, neutral, or negative charge.
- ~ Your thoughts give off a vibrational frequency and fuel your feelings. Your feelings are e-motions or "energy in motion."
- ~ Those emotions trigger responses in your central nervous system automatically.
- ~ Your brain gives off electrical impulses.
- ~ The heart is a magnetic field that is always radiating energy.
- ~ Your body creates chemical and hormonal reactions that create coherence or incoherence throughout your body.
- ~ Your mind serves the body with those chemical reactions and instructions to survive.

- ~ Your body's reaction to stress is known as the "fight or flight" nervous response.
- ~ Human beings are not meant to live in a constant state of stress which causes disease or illness.
- ~ Over time, your body becomes your unconscious program.
- ~ Your actions or reactions turn into habits.
- ~ Your habits turn into your behaviors.
- ~ Your behaviors become your personality.
- ~ Your personality reflects your personal reality.
- ~ Your personality is based on your viewpoint or perspective.
- ~ Your perspective shapes your worldview.
- ~ Your worldview affects your *Life Timeline*.
- ~ Your *Life Timeline* is composed of a series of present moments, experienced over the course of the years you have been alive in this physical body.
- ~ Every second is a present moment—your opportunity to change.
- ~ You hold the power to affect your internal and external environment any second through your consciousness.
- ~ Your consciousness is your attention or awareness.
- ~ Your screen is the veil between the conscious and subconscious mind.
- ~ The screen is your perspective.
- ~ The program operates based on your perspective at the time of inception.
- ~ You can flip your screen.
- ~ Where you place your attention is where your energy flows.
- ~ Focus on what you want.
- ~ Fear limits your power.

- Social conditioning exists. Be aware of your program.
- Space and time have no structure unless you provide it.
- Your observation collapses waves of probability into particles of creation.
- Life is a journey of evolution every day.
- Consciousness allows you to connect to your power.
- Thoughts become things.
- Your feelings affect your actions.
- Your actions become your results.
- If you don't like your results, you need to notice your way of thinking.
- Love and faith carry a higher vibrational frequency than hate and fear.
- Choose love in all you do.
- Practice forgiveness—it frees you.
- Allow your soul to sing while pursuing your passion.
- Take action, daily. Baby steps will take you up that mountain quicker than you think.
- You have a dream or yearning for more for a reason.
- You are capable of anything you put your mind to.
- Believe in the power of source energy.
- Believe in miracles and celebrate each time you manifest one.
- Your dream is worthy you and you are worthy of it.
- Fertilize your soil so the seeds can take root.
- Be mindful of the energy you give off as well as the energy you receive from others.
- Remember that energy cannot be created or destroyed, only transformed.
- Breakthrough the bonds of your past and step into the light of love.
- Opportunity and infinite possibility exist.

- ∼ Claim it.
- ∼ Speak it, act on it, and repeat.
- ∼ Celebrate the new YOU... *"This or something even greater still... and **so it is.**"*

The Voice of Truth

During a commencement speech at Stanford University, in 2005, Steve Jobs said:

> *Your time is limited, so don't waste it living someone else's life. Don't be trapped by dogma... living with the results of other people's thinking. Don't let the noise of others' opinions drown out your own inner voice. And most important, have the courage to follow your heart and intuition.*[86]

Are you willing to listen to your intuition? What is it saying to you right now? That silent insight or knowing—it's your sixth sense. It tries to give you guidance (like an internal GPS) through the invisible jungle of energetic vibration. It's able to decipher the information in the Quantum Field to offer the inkling or feeling you sense. Listen to it. Talk to it. You can ask your intuition questions. Why am I so blessed and abundant? Why am I so lucky to have so many people who love and support me? When you ask questions from this perspective, the ego isn't able to interpret or interrupt them. Ask fulfilling questions before you go to bed at night and expect to receive signals in some way. The Universe speaks through many channels, so always be on the lookout for cues and clues to help aid your transformation.

Take action on your goals every day without fearing, doubting, or worrying about the outcome. Trust in the truth you have uncovered and allow it to rinse you clean as you practice the *7-Step Life Timeline System of Transformation*. If you have a hard time following through and completing your goals, invest in the coaching program and get support to ensure your success. Isn't each present moment for the rest of your life worth it? Your relationships? Happiness? Your health? You can positively influence your loved ones and other people around you. You can have an impact on the whole—your evolution expands consciousness. Rise up above the screened viewpoint, reach over the mountain of fear, and take hold of the confidence and peace offered by your new perspective. Get out of the matrix.

Tag it.
Remember it.
Feel it.
Flip it.
Release it.
Reprogram.
Resonate.
RINSE & REPEAT!

It's Your Time

Einstein said, "Everything is energy and that's all there is to it. Match the frequency of the reality you want and you cannot help but get that reality. It can be no other way. This is not philosophy. This is physics."[87] He was a brilliant man and I'm grateful for the insight he shared with us. Insight that can help us navigate the intricacies and vast probabilities of this Universe.

    I reflect on this system of transformation and the principles of the program daily. As a result, my consciousness rises and allows me to see opportunities to co-create my reality. Every day, I tag self-defeating thoughts or unconscious, self-sabotaging tendencies and override their power by shifting my mindset. I don't engage in the negative news or the media frenzy about the virus or vaccination requirements. My faith is much stronger than the fear they impose upon us. I stopped trying to find a man to love me. Instead, I focused on loving my son and myself. When I found my true self, let down my walls, and overcame my subconscious programming, the right people started showing up in my life. Opportunities and synchronicities were delivered to my doorstep, and so was the man of my dreams. I was open to the portal of opportunity for love. In other words, I resonated with the energetic frequency of love and in doing so, I invited love into my life. Unexpectantly, I met my soulmate on my front porch. He came to my house to give me a price quote to install skylights in my living room. We talked about energy and the power of our minds. We connected on so many levels instantaneously. Now, we are madly in love with one another. His kiss sends electricity through every cell in my body. Remember my vision in Chapter 13? Well, I manifested it into reality! We laugh, cry, and share our truth with each other. He is my best friend and the soulmate I had been so eager to meet. When I became conscious of what I truly wanted, it showed up in perfect form. I have a burning desire for our future together and a grateful expectation that all our dreams will come to fruition—this or something even greater still.

    If you overcome your own mind and do the work required, I promise you, it's more than worth it. This system can transform your life, affecting your relationships, enhancing others' lives, and people along the way. If you want to be a part of positive change, you need to start with yourself. You are a part of the whole. The sooner we all realize this and take action steps to improve our lives, the sooner we will see the effects ripple through the Universe.

All the years I spent yearning and searching for the love of my life were spent in limbo. I needed to love myself first. I needed to feel complete and find happiness, because a man could never complete or fill the void inside me. I needed to fill it with love and practice forgiveness. Once you override your faulty programming, you allow the Universe to deliver the partner that makes sense to complete your puzzle.

The most rewarding experiences usually come after tough and trying times, but maybe that's what it takes to wake us up from the egoic distractions of our finite world. Tyson, the love of my life always says, "It's all about timing." I truly believe that now. What happens during your *life timeline* is influenced by your level of consciousness. Oftentimes, it takes *time* to gain a clear perspective to shift your life path. We are born into our bodies perfect. Every baby is perfect. Then we become conditioned, and life happens between the rise and fall of it all. We see a finite world. However, we all long for something greater and sense there is much more to be discovered. This is a sense that unites humanity. The quantum worldview and scientific breakthroughs of the twenty-first century are just beginning to show us the power we hold. As your level of consciousness rises, so does your ability to connect with your higher self, align with faith, and awaken to the truth. Awareness gives humanity power to shift our realities. It's your time to wake up from the conditions of your past, override the fear and worry, and take hold of your greatness. Connect to the spirit driven life force you hold and co-create a life that you love. Choose to have a positive influence on those around you and the world at large. When more people wake up, rise up, and start speaking up, we become consciously connected to make this world a better place!

Connect to your power, unconditional love, and Source energy. Believe and achieve. It's your time. Time to fulfill **your soul's purpose!**

As I was preparing to finalize this book, I decided to draw a bath and allow my intuition to speak to me while relaxing in the warm, intellectual, cleansing water. Dr. Masaru Emoto, a Japanese pseudoscientist and author, discovered that water holds a great deal of power and information. "Emoto said that water was a 'blueprint for our reality' and that emotional 'energies' and 'vibrations' could change its physical structure."[88] People flock to oceans and lakes, I believe, because water offers insight and divine cleansing properties. You may notice that your best ideas come to you in the shower or during a bath. The following insight came directly from my intuition as I relaxed into my nice warm bath—her spirit told me to leave you with this...

> Go draw a bath with nice, warm, loving water.
> Add some Epsom salts or your favorite bubble bath.
> Light a few candles. Invite the light in.
> Put on some spa relaxation music (look for this on YouTube and select the first one that resonates with you).

BEHIND THE SCREEN

Connect your Bluetooth speaker, if you have one.
Pour a glass of wine. (If you prefer).
Test the water temperature before getting in. ☺
Allow your body to soak into the refreshing water. Just relax.
Listen to the peaceful music and quiet your mind.
Focus on your breathing and feel gratitude for all you have.
Allow your intuition to lead the way.
It will guide you, once you allow it, into some beautiful bright places...

~ Insight.
~ Inspiration.
~ Ideas.

Let your intuition come alive and guide you. Through your consciousness, you have the power. Your truth lies *behind the screen. This or something even greater still....*

Stay tuned for *Behind the Screen* – Part 2.

Thank you for reading this book. I hope it makes a difference in your life and I wish you infinite blessings on your transformational journey. If you enjoyed reading, please leave a review on the retailer's website where you purchased this book. I read every review and they help new readers discover my books.

With infinite love and peace,

Carrie L. Schmidt

Take your *Life Timeline* reflection to the next level by enrolling in the supplemental 12-week coaching program, **Master your Mind & Heal your Soul.** Visit www.carrie-schmidt.com for more information.

About the Author

As the Founder and CEO of Infinite SOULutions, LLC, Carrie Schmidt puts the *SOUL* in *SOUL*utions by transforming lives personally and professionally. She is a dynamic, influential

BEHIND THE SCREEN

Thought Leader and Motivational Speaker who has the ability to instantly captivate your mind, heart and awaken your soul by empowering you to gain clarity of your purpose in life, overcome limiting beliefs, and gain the confidence to step outside your comfort zone. She customizes her approach to each clients' needs and teaches the tools required to actually transform their personal or professional goals into reality.

Carrie teaches a structured system of transformation that has helped her transform her own life and now has a significant impact on others' lives. Having done all of this herself, as a single mom at age 25 on welfare and barely making it by, Carrie vowed to provide the best life for her son. She entered corporate America working an entry level position in Customer Service and swiftly climbed the ladder in management by showcasing her talents for problem solving, teambuilding, and conscious leadership. After 10 years of dedicated hard work, Carrie assumed full P&L responsibility for a $100 million unionized manufacturing facility as General Manager. Within 3 months of being promoted to this position, a woman in a mostly male-dominated industry, she led the team to record breaking improvements.

After achieving everything she ever worked for, Carrie still felt a longing for something greater. She embarked on a spiritual journey of personal discovery and development that led her to research the fundamentals of psychology, neuroscience and quantum physics. She ventured to Los Angeles and studied under Mary Morrissey at the Life Mastery Institute to become a Certified Life Mastery Consultant. It became her passion to help raise human consciousness and teach what she learned as an adult to teens and young adults who need to understand the power of the mind.

Now, considered an Enterprise Change Agent and Transformational Thought Leader, Carrie offers life coaching

ABOUT THE AUTHOR

programs, business consulting services, and is releasing her first book, Behind the Screen, which teaches the *7-Step Life Timeline System of Transformation*. Her vision is to reach, teach, and transform over 1 million lives globally by helping raise human consciousness.

A Special Thanks to my Sponsors:

Thank you for believing in my dream and supporting Behind the Screen.

Dan Foy

Renata Kuhns Coaching LLC

Lindsay Andreotti and Brilliance Enterprises

Brad Robinson from KaiZenergy.net

Bibliography

Allen, James. *As a Man Thinketh*. Mount Vernon, N.Y.: Peter Pauper Press, 1951.

Bromley, D. Allan. *A Century of Physics*. New York: Springer New York, 2013.

Canfield, Jack. *The Key to Living the Law of Attraction: The Secret to Creating the Life of Your Dreams.* London: Orion, 2014.

Chopra, Deepak. *What Are You Hungry For? The Chopra Solution to Permanent Weight Loss, Well-Being, and Lightness of Soul.* New York: Potter/Ten Speed/Harmony/Rodale, 2014.

Dispenza, Joe. *Breaking The Habit of Being Yourself: How to Lose Your Mind and Create a New One.* London: Hay House, 2013.

Seuss, Dr. *Happy Birthday to You!* New York: Random House Children's Books, 2013.

Dyer, Wayne W. *The Power of Intention: Learning to Co-create Your World Your Way:* Easyread Super Large 20pt Edition. n.p.: CreateSpace, 2009.

Goddard, Neville. *The Neville Collection: All 10 Books by a Modern Master.* n.c.: Independently Published by the Neville Collection, 2020.

Hawkins, David R. *The Map of Consciousness Explained: A Proven Energy Scale to Actualize Your Ultimate Potential.* United States: Hay House, 2020.

Hebb, D.O. *The Organization of Behavior.* New York: Wiley & Sons, 1949.

Heriot, Drew, director. Rhonda Byrne, producer. *The Secret.* Prime Time Productions, 2006.

Hill, Napoleon. *Think and Grow Rich.* New York: Fawcett Crest, 1987.

Hollis, Rachel. *Girl, Wash Your Face: Stop Believing the Lies About Who You Are So You Can Become Who You Were Meant to Be.* Nashville: Thomas Nelson, 2018.

Holliwell, Raymond. *Working with the Law: 11 Truth Principles for Successful Living.* Camarillo, CA: DeVorss Publications, 2005.

Murphy, Joseph. *The Power of Your Subconscious Mind: The Complete Original Edition.* New York: St. Martin's Publishing Group, 2019.

BIBLIOGRAPHY

Nelson, Dr. Bradley. *The Emotion Code: How to Release Your Trapped Emotions for Abundant Health, Love, and Happiness* (Updated and Expanded Edition). New York: St. Martin's Publishing Group, 2019.

Pennebaker, James W. *Opening Up, Second Edition: The Healing Power of Expressing Emotions*. London: Guilford Publications, 1997.

Pert, Candace B. *Molecules of Emotion: The Science Behind Mind-Body Medicine*. London: Scribner, 1999.

Reddy, M S. "Depression: The Disorder and the Burden." *Indian Journal of Psychological Medicine*. vol. 32,1. (2010): 1-2. doi:10.4103/0253-7176.70510.

Schucman, Helen. *A Course in Miracles:* Combined Volume (Third Edition). Mill Valley, CA: Foundation for Inner Peace, 2007.

Substance Abuse and Mental Health Services Administration. (2021). Key substance use and mental health indicators in the United States: Results from the 2020 National Survey on Drug Use and Health (HHS Publication No. PEP21-07-01-003, NSDUH Series H-56). Rockville, MD: Center for Behavioral Health Statistics and Quality, Substance Abuse and Mental Health Services Administration. Retrieved from https://www.samhsa.gov/data/.

Three Initiates. *The Kybalion: A Study of the Hermetic Philosophy of Ancient Egypt and Greece.* Chicago: The Yogi Publication Society, 1908.

Tolle, Eckhart. *A New Earth: Awakening to Your Life's Purpose*. London: Penguin Publishing Group, 2008.

Williamson, Marianne. *A Course in Weight Loss: 21 Spiritual Lessons for Surrendering Your Weight Forever*. New York City: Hay House, 2012.

Zukav, Gary. *The Seat of the Soul*. London: Simon & Schuster, 2007.

URLs

"Gautama Buddha Quotes." AZ Quotes. Accessed Jan. 11, 2021. https://www.azquotes.com/quote/668538.

"821 Angel Number – Meaning and Symbolism." Angel Number. Accessed August 21, 2021. https://angelnumber.org/821-angel-number-meaning-and-symbolism/.

"85 Famous Filling A Void In Your Life Quotes." Quotes to Spark. Nov. 5, 2020. https://quotestospark.com/filling-a-void-in-your-life-quotes/.

"9 Ways Crying May Benefit Your Health." Healthline. Accessed Jan. 11, 2021. https://www.healthline.com/health/benefits-of-crying#selfsoothing.

"Albert Einstein Quotes." Quote Fancy. Accessed January 10, 2021. https://quotefancy.com/quote/763343/Albert-Einstein-Everything-is-Energy-and-that-is-all-there-is-to-it-Match-the-frequency.

"Bullying Statistics." Pacer's National Bullying Prevention Center. (2019). Accessed June 20, 2021. https://www.pacer.org/bullying/info/stats.asp.

"Carl Sagan." In *Oxford Essential Quotations*, edited by Ratcliffe, Susan. Oxford University Press. https://www.oxfordreference.com/view/10.1093/acref/9780191826719.001.0001/q-oro-ed4-00009067.

"consciousness." Merriam-Webster.com Dictionary, s.v. Accessed January 11, 2022. https://www.merriam-webster.com/dictionary/consciousness.

"Earl Nightingale Motivational Quotes." AZ Quotes. Accessed January 11, 2021. https://www.azquotes.com/author/10824-Earl_Nightingale/tag/motivational.

"Gary Zukav Quotes." Goodreads. Accessed Jan. 1, 2021. https://www.goodreads.com/author/quotes/26975.Gary_Zukav.

"George Bernard Shaw Quotes." Goodreads. Accessed December 4, 2021. https://www.goodreads.com/quotes/87185-progress-is-impossible-without-change-and-those-who-cannot-change.

"Henry David Thoreau Quotes." Goodreads. Accessed January 11, 2021. https://www.goodreads.com/quotes/10280670-it-is-the-beauty-within-us-that-makes-it-possible.

"Henry David Thoreau Quotes." KEEPINSPIRING.ME. Accessed Jan. 11, 2021. https://www.keepinspiring.me/henry-david-thoreau-quotes/.

URLS

"How many Earths? How many countries?" Earth Overshot Day. Accessed December 1, 2021. https://www.overshootday.org/how-many-earths-or-countries-do-we-need/.

"Joseph Campbell Quotes: What each must seek in his life…" Inspirational Stories. Accessed January 11, 2021. https://www.inspirationalstories.com/quotes/joseph-campbell-what-each-must-seek-in-his-life/.

"Light-energy meaning." Your Dictionary. Accessed December 4, 2020. https://www.yourdictionary.com/light-energy.

"Mahatma Gandhi Quotes." Goodreads. Accessed Jan. 11, 2021. https://www.goodreads.com/quotes/50584-your-beliefs-become-your-thoughts-your-thoughts-become-your-words.

"Marianne Williamson Quotes." Goodreads. Accessed Jan. 11, 2021. https://www.goodreads.com/author/quotes/17297.Marianne_Williamson.

"Mary Morrissey." Brave Thinking Institute. Accessed Jan. 11, 2021. https://www.bravethinkinginstitute.com/faculty/mary-morrissey.

"Maya Angelou Quotes." AZ Quotes. Accessed Jan. 11, 2021. https://www.azquotes.com/quote/344894.

"Nikola Tesla Quotes." Goodreads. Accessed December 1, 2021. https://www.goodreads.com/quotes/361785-if-you-want-to-find-the-secrets-of-the-universe.

"Ralph Waldo Emerson Quotes." Lib Quotes. Accessed Jan. 11, 2021. https://libquotes.com/ralph-waldo-emerson.

"The Fractal Foundation." The Albert I Pierce Foundation. Accessed December 15, 2021. http://www.aipfoundation.org/fractal-foundation-grant.html.

"The Holstee Manifesto." Holstee. Accessed December 6, 2021. https://www.holstee.com/pages/manifesto.

"The Secret Plot Summary." IMBd. Accessed December 5, 2021. https://www.imdb.com/title/tt0846789/plotsummary

"To Withhold Forgiveness." The Catholic Storeroom. Accessed Jan. 11, 2021. http://www.catholicstoreroom.com/category/quotes/quote-author/augustine-354-430/page/30/.

"Tyler Perry Quotes." Success Story. Accessed Jan. 11, 2021. https://successstory.com/quote/tyler-perry.

"Understanding brain waves." Neurofeedback Alliance. Accessed December 4, 2021. https://neurofeedbackalliance.org/understanding-brain-waves/.

"Vincent van Gogh Quotes." AZ Quotes. Accessed Jan. 11, 2021. https://www.azquotes.com/quote/494807.

"Warning Signs of Mental Illness." American Psychiatric Association. Accessed December 4, 2021. https://www.psychiatry.org/patients-families/warning-signs-of-mental-illness.

URLS

"Wayne Dyer Quotes About Past." AZ Quotes. Accessed Dec. 1, 2021. https://www.azquotes.com/author/4269-Wayne_Dyer/tag/past.

"What Is Mental Illness?" American Psychiatric Association. Accessed December 4, 2021. https://www.psychiatry.org/patients-families/what-is-mental-illness.

"What is the Mind-Body Connection?" Earl E. Bakken Center for Spirituality and Healing – Taking Charge of Your Health & Wellbeing. Accessed December 4, 2021. https://www.taking-charge.csh.umn.edu/what-is-the-mind-body-connection.

Berger, Christine and Susan K. Thompson. "Biofield Therapies." ACA COUNSELING CORNER BLOG. June 12, 2019. https://www.counseling.org/news/aca-blogs/aca-counseling-corner/aca-member-blogs/2019/06/12/biofield-therapies.

Britannica, T. Editors of Encyclopedia. "mind." Encyclopedia Britannica. August 5, 2016. https://www.britannica.com/topic/mind.

Burkholder, Liz. Burkholder Wellness. Charlotte, NC. http://burkholderwellness.com/.

Centers for Disease Control and Prevention. National Center for Injury Prevention and Control. Web-based Injury Statistics Query and Reporting System (WISQARS) [online]. (May 2021). Retrieved from https://www.cdc.gov/injury/wisqars/.

Cherry, Kendra. "How Experience Changes Brain Plasticity." Updated February 3, 2021. https://www.verywellmind.com/what-is-brain-plasticity-2794886.

Colman, Andrew M. *A Dictionary of Psychology*. 3rd ed. Oxford University Press. 2009. https://www.oxfordreference.com/view/10.1093/acref/9780199534067.001.0001/acref-9780199534067.

Gaia Staff. "Simple Tapping Technique Found to Lower Stress, Boost Immunity." Gaia. December 23, 2021. https://www.gaia.com/article/eft-tapping.

Ghosh, Iman. "Which Companies Belong to the Elite Trillion-Dollar Club?" Visual Capitalist. Visual Capitalist. August 23, 2021. https://www.visualcapitalist.com/which-companies-belong-to-the-elite-trillion-dollar-club/.

Harvard Medical School. 2007. National Comorbidity Survey (NCS). (2017, August 21). Retrieved from https://www.hcp.med.harvard.edu/ncs/index.php. Data Table 2: 12-month prevalence DSM-IV/WMH-CIDI disorders by sex and cohort.

Herculano-Houzel, Suzana. "The Human Brain in Numbers: A Linearly Scaled-up Primate Brain." Frontiers in Human Neuroscience. 3, no. 31. (2009): Accessed December 4, 2021. https://www.ncbi.nlm.nih.gov/pmc/articles/PMC2776484/.

Iqbal, Mansoor. "Fortnite Usage and Revenue Statistics (2022)." Business of Apps. n.p. January 11, 2022. https://www.businessofapps.com/data/fortnite-statistics/.

URLS

Jobs, Steve. "'YOUR TIME IS LIMITED, SO DON'T WASTE IT LIVING SOMEONE ELSE'S LIFE': JOBS." First Post. October 06, 2011. https://www.firstpost.com/tech/news-analysis/your-time-is-limited-so-dont-waste-it-living-someone-elses-life-jobs-2-3589139.html.

Kamrath, Sarah. "Happy Healthy Child: A Holistic Approach." February 8, 2012. https://www.brucelipton.com/happy-healthy-child-holistic-approach/.

Kidadl Team. "41 Max Planck Quotes from the Nobel Prize Winner and Father of Quantum Physics." Last modified November 14, 2021. https://kidadl.com/articles/max-planck-quotes-from-the-nobel-prize-winner-and-father-of-quantum-physics.

Leman, Jennifer. "A Quantum Leap in the Classical World." Popular Mechanics. October 2, 2019. https://www.popularmechanics.com/science/math/a29339863/quantum-superposition-molecules/.

Patel, Jainish and Prittesh Patel. "Consequences of Repression of Emotion: Physical Health, Mental Health and General Well Being." International Journal of Psychotherapy Practice and Research – 2019. https://openaccesspub.org/ijpr/article/999#ridm1850271412.

Perkowitz, S. "E = mc2." Encyclopedia Britannica. July 22, 2021. https://www.britannica.com/science/E-mc2-equation.

Raypole, Crystal. "Let It Out: Dealing With Repressed Emotions." Healthline. Last modified March 31, 2020.

https://www.healthline.com/health/repressed-emotions#physical-effects.

Sanders, Bernie. "How Corporate Media Threatens our Democracy." Last modified January 26, 2017. https://inthesetimes.com/features/bernie-sanders-corporate-media-threatens-our-democracy.html.

Stapleton, P., J. Dispenza, S. McGill, D. Sabot, M. Peach, D. Raynor. "Large effects of brief meditation intervention on EEG spectra in meditation novices." *IBRO Reports*. Volume 9, (2020): 290-301. ISSN 2451-8301. https://doi.org/10.1016/j.ibror.2020.10.006.

Tracy, Brian. "Subconscious Mind Power Explained." Brian Tracy International (blog). Accessed November 20, 2021. https://www.briantracy.com/blog/personal-success/understanding-your-subconscious-mind/.

Wikipedia contributors. "Andrew Carnegie." Wikipedia, The Free Encyclopedia. Accessed December 8, 2021. https://en.wikipedia.org/wiki/Andrew_Carnegie.

Wikipedia contributors. "As above, so below." Wikipedia, The Free Encyclopedia. Last modified January 26, 2022. https://en.wikipedia.org/w/index.php?title=As_above,_so_below&oldid=1067971621.

Wikipedia contributors. "Frequency." Wikipedia, The Free Encyclopedia. Accessed January 1, 2021. https://en.wikipedia.org/wiki/Frequency.

URLS

Wikipedia contributors. "Masaru Emoto." Wikipedia, The Free Encyclopedia. Accessed February 10, 2022. https://en.wikipedia.org/w/index.php?title=Masaru_Emoto&oldid=1070271157.

Endnotes

[1] Virginia Woolf, *Three Guineas*: First edition (New York: Harvest Books, 2006), 16.

[2] Helen Schucman, *A Course in Miracles: Combined Volume* (Third Edition) (Mill Valley, CA: Foundation for Inner Peace, 2007).

[3] Dr. Seuss, *Happy Birthday to You!* (New York: Random House Children's Books, 2013).

[4] Joseph Murphy, *The Power of Your Subconscious Mind:* The Complete Original Edition (New York: St. Martin's Publishing Group, 2019) Ch. 1.

[5] "mind," *Encyclopedia Britannica*, August 5, 2016, https://www.britannica.com/topic/mind.

[6] D.O. Hebb, *The Organization of Behavior*. New York: Wiley & Sons, 1949.

[7] Brian Tracy, "Subconscious Mind Power Explained," Brian Tracy International (blog), accessed November 20, 2021, https://www.briantracy.com/blog/personal-success/understanding-your-subconscious-mind/.

[8] Andrew M. Colman, *A Dictionary of Psychology*, 3rd ed. Oxford University Press, 2009, https://www.oxfordreference.com/view/10.1093/acref/9780199534067.001.0001/acref-9780199534067.

[9] Suzana Herculano-Houzel, "The Human Brain in Numbers: A Linearly Scaled-up Primate Brain," Frontiers in Human Neuroscience, 3, no. 31, (2009): accessed December 4, 2021. https://www.ncbi.nlm.nih.gov/pmc/articles/PMC2776484/.

[10] "What Is the Mind-Body Connection," Earl E. Bakken Center for Spirituality and Healing Taking Charge of Your Health & Wellbeing, accessed December 4, 2021, https://www.takingcharge.csh.umn.edu/what-is-the-mind-body-connection.

[11] Sarah Kamrath, "Happy Healthy Child: A Holistic Approach," February 8, 2012, https://www.brucelipton.com/happy-healthy-child-holistic-approach/.

[12] "Understanding brain waves," Neurofeedback Alliance, accessed December 4, 2021, https://neurofeedbackalliance.org/understanding-brain-waves/.

[13] Ibid.

[14] Bernie Sanders, "How Corporate Media Threatens our Democracy," last modified January 26, 2017, https://inthesetimes.com/features/bernie-sanders-corporate-media-threatens-our-democracy.html.

[15] Mansoor Iqbal, "Fortnite Usage and Revenue Statistics (2022)," Business of Apps, n.p., January 11, 2022, https://www.businessofapps.com/data/fortnite-statistics/.

[16] Iman Ghosh, "Which Companies Belong to the Elite Trillion-Dollar Club?," Visual Capitalist, Visual Capitalist, August 23, 2021, https://www.visualcapitalist.com/which-companies-belong-to-the-elite-trillion-dollar-club/.

[17] Deepak Chopra, *What Are You Hungry For? The Chopra Solution to Permanent Weight Loss, Well-Being, and Lightness of Soul* (New York: Potter/Ten Speed/Harmony/Rodale, 2014), Part 2.

[18] Wikipedia contributors, "As above, so below." Wikipedia, The Free Encyclopedia, last modified January 26, 2022, https://en.wikipedia.org/w/index.php?title=As_above,_so_below&oldid=1067971621.

[19] Three Initiates, *The Kybalion: A Study of the Hermetic Philosophy of Ancient Egypt and Greece (Chicago: The Yogi Publication Society, 1908)*, 22-30.

[20] "Gautama Buddha Quotes," AZ Quotes, accessed Jan. 11, 2021, https://www.azquotes.com/quote/668538.

[21] "Carl Sagan," in *Oxford Essential Quotations*, edited by Susan Ratcliffe, Oxford University Press, https://www.oxfordreference.com/view/10.1093/acref/9780191826719.001.0001/q-oro-ed4-00009067.

[22] "Henry David Thoreau Quotes," KEEPINSPIRING.ME, accessed Jan. 11, 2021. https://www.keepinspiring.me/henry-david-thoreau-quotes/.

[23] Helen Schucman, *A Course in Miracles*, 11.

[24] "Earl Nightingale Motivational Quotes," AZ Quotes, accessed January 11, 2021. https://www.azquotes.com/author/10824-Earl_Nightingale/tag/motivational.

ENDNOTES

[25] "85 Famous Filling A Void In Your Life Quotes," Quotes to Spark, Nov. 5, 2020, https://quotestospark.com/filling-a-void-in-your-life-quotes/.

[26] "Ralph Waldo Emerson Quotes," Lib Quotes, accessed Jan. 11, 2021, https://libquotes.com/ralph-waldo-emerson.

[27] "Henry David Thoreau Quotes," Goodreads, accessed January 11, 2021, https://www.goodreads.com/quotes/10280670-it-is-the-beauty-within-us-that-makes-it-possible.

[28] "How many Earths? How many countries?," Earth Overshot Day, accessed December 1, 2021, https://www.overshootday.org/how-many-earths-or-countries-do-we-need/.

[29] Centers for Disease Control and Prevention, National Center for Injury Prevention and Control, Web-based Injury Statistics Query and Reporting System (WISQARS) [online], May 2021, Retrieved from https://www.cdc.gov/injury/wisqars.

[30] Substance Abuse and Mental Health Services Administration. (2021). Key substance use and mental health indicators in the United States: Results from the 2020 National Survey on Drug Use and Health (HHS Publication No. PEP21-07-01-003, NSDUH Series H-56). Rockville, MD: Center for Behavioral Health Statistics and Quality, Substance Abuse and Mental Health Services Administration. Retrieved from https://www.samhsa.gov/data/.

[31] Ibid.

[32] "Bullying Statistics," Pacer's National Bullying Prevention Center, (2019), Accessed June 20, 2021, https://www.pacer.org/bullying/info/stats.asp.

[33] Ibid.

[34] M S. Reddy, "Depression: The Disorder and the Burden," Indian Journal of Psychological Medicine, vol. 32,1. (2010): 1-2. doi:10.4103/0253-7176.70510.

[35] Harvard Medical School, 2007, National Comorbidity Survey (NCS), (2017, August 21), Retrieved from https://www.hcp.med.harvard.edu/ncs/index.php. Data Table 2: 12-month prevalence DSM-IV/WMH-CIDI disorders by sex and cohort.

36 "Warning Signs of Mental Illness," American Psychiatric Association, accessed December 4, 2021, https://www.psychiatry.org/patients-families/warning-signs-of-mental-illness.

37 "What Is Mental Illness?" American Psychiatric Association, accessed December 4, 2021, https://www.psychiatry.org/patients-families/what-is-mental-illness.

38 "The Fractal Foundation," The Albert I Pierce Foundation, accessed December 15, 2021, http://www.aipfoundation.org/fractal-foundation-grant.html.

39 Allan D. Bromley, *A Century of Physics* (New York: Springer New York, 2013), 47.

40 James Allen, *As a Man Thinketh* (Mount Vernon, N.Y.: Peter Pauper Press, 1951).

41 Neville Goddard, *The Neville Collection - All 10 Books by a Modern Master* (n.c.: Independently Published by the Neville Collection, 2020), 40.

42 Ibid, 43.

43 Sidney Perkowitz, "E = mc2," Encyclopedia Britannica, July 22, 2021, https://www.britannica.com/science/E-mc2-equation.

44 "consciousness," Merriam-Webster.com Dictionary, s.v., accessed January 11, 2022, https://www.merriam-webster.com/dictionary/consciousness.

45 "Light-energy meaning," Your Dictionary, accessed December 4, 2020, https://www.yourdictionary.com/light-energy.

46 "Nicola Tesla Quotes," Goodreads, accessed December 1, 2021, https://www.goodreads.com/quotes/361785-if-you-want-to-find-the-secrets-of-the-universe.

47 Ibid.

48 Jennifer Leman, "A Quantum Leap in the Classical World," Popular Mechanics, October 2, 2019, https://www.popularmechanics.com/science/math/a29339863/quantum-superposition-molecules/.

49 Three Initiates, *The Kybalion: A Study of the Hermetic Philosophy of Ancient Egypt and Greece* (Chicago: The Yogi Publication Society, 1908), 32.

ENDNOTES

50 Christine Berger, Susan K. Thompson, "Biofield Therapies," ACA COUNSELING CORNER BLOG, June 12, 2019, https://www.counseling.org/news/aca-blogs/aca-counseling-corner/aca-member-blogs/2019/06/12/biofield-therapies.

51 John 14:20 (KJV)

52 Exo 3:14 (KJV)

53 "George Bernard Shaw Quotes," Goodreads, accessed December 4, 2021, https://www.goodreads.com/quotes/87185-progress-is-impossible-without-change-and-those-who-cannot-change.

54 Helen Schucman, xi.

55 Kidadl Team, "41 Max Planck Quotes From The Nobel Prize Winner And Father Of Quantum Physics," last modified November 14, 2021, https://kidadl.com/articles/max-planck-quotes-from-the-nobel-prize-winner-and-father-of-quantum-physics.

56 "Wayne Dyer Quotes About Past," AZ Quotes, accessed Dec. 1, 2021, https://www.azquotes.com/author/4269-Wayne_Dyer/tag/past.

57 "Vincent van Gogh Quotes," AZ Quotes, accessed Jan. 11, 2021, https://www.azquotes.com/quote/494807.

58 "821 Angel Number – Meaning and Symbolism," Angel Number, accessed August 21, 2021, https://angelnumber.org/821-angel-number-meaning-and-symbolism/.

59 "Sigmund Freud Quotes," Goodreads, accessed January 6, 2021, https://www.goodreads.com/author/quotes/10017.Sigmund_Freud.

60 Candace B. Pert, *Molecules of Emotion: The Science Behind Mind-Body Medicine (London: Scribner, 1999).*

61 Dr. Bradley Nelson, *The Emotion Code: How to Release Your Trapped Emotions for Abundant Health, Love, and Happiness* (Updated and Expanded Edition) (New York: St. Martin's Publishing Group, 2019).

62 Jainish Patel, Prittesh Patel, "Consequences of Repression of Emotion: Physical Health, Mental Health and General Well Being," 1(3):16-21, International Journal of Psychotherapy Practice and Research – 2019, https://openaccesspub.org/ijpr/article/999#ridm1850271412.

63 Crystal Raypole. "Let It Out: Dealing With Repressed Emotions," Healthline, last modified March 31, 2020, https://www.healthline.com/health/repressed-emotions#physical-effects.

⁶⁴ Gaia Staff, "Simple Tapping Technique Found to Lower Stress, Boost Immunity," Gaia, December 23, 2021, https://www.gaia.com/article/eft-tapping.

⁶⁵ "9 Ways Crying May Benefit Your Health," Healthline, accessed Jan. 11, 2021, https://www.healthline.com/health/benefits-of-crying#-selfsoothing.

⁶⁶ P. Stapleton, J. Dispenza, S. McGill, D. Sabot, M. Peach, D. Raynor, Large effects of brief meditation intervention on EEG spectra in meditation novices, IBRO Reports, Volume 9, 2020, Pages 290-301, ISSN 2451-8301, https://doi.org/10.1016/j.ibror.2020.10.006.

⁶⁷ "To Withhold Forgiveness," The Catholic Storeroom, accessed Jan. 11, 2021, http://www.catholicstoreroom.com/category/quotes/quote-author/augustine-354-430/page/30/.

⁶⁸ "Tyler Perry Quotes," Success Story, accessed Jan. 11, 2021, https://successstory.com/quote/tyler-perry.

⁶⁹ James W. Pennebaker, *Opening Up, Second Edition: The Healing Power of Expressing Emotions* (London: Guilford Publications, 1997).

⁷⁰ Eckhart Tolle, *A New Earth: Awakening to Your Life's Purpose* (London: Penguin Publishing Group, 2008).

⁷¹ "Marianne Williamson Quotes," Goodreads, accessed Jan. 11, 2021, https://www.goodreads.com/author/quotes/17297.Marianne_Williamson.

⁷² Jack Canfield, *The Key to Living the Law of Attraction: The Secret to Creating the Life of Your Dreams* (London: Orion, 2014), 139.

⁷³ "Mahatma Gandhi Quotes," Goodreads, accessed Jan. 11, 2021, https://www.goodreads.com/quotes/50584-your-beliefs-become-your-thoughts-your-thoughts-become-your-words.

⁷⁴ Kendra Cherry, "How Experience Changes Brain Plasticity," updated February 3, 2021, https://www.verywellmind.com/what-is-brain-plasticity-2794886.

⁷⁵ "Mary Morrissey," Brave Thinking Institute, accessed Jan. 11, 2021, https://www.bravethinkinginstitute.com/faculty/mary-morrissey.

⁷⁶ Marianne Williamson, *A Course in Weight Loss: 21 Spiritual Lessons for Surrendering Your Weight Forever* (New York City: Hay House, 2012), 158.

ENDNOTES

[77] "Joseph Campbell Quotes: What each must seek in his life…," Inspirational Stories, accessed January 11, 2021, https://www.inspirationalstories.com/quotes/joseph-campbell-what-each-must-seek-in-his-life/.

[78] Wikipedia contributors, "Frequency," Wikipedia, The Free Encyclopedia, accessed January 1, 2021, https://en.wikipedia.org/wiki/Frequency.

[79] David R. Hawkins, *The Map of Consciousness Explained: A Proven Energy Scale to Actualize Your Ultimate Potential* (United States: Hay House, 2020).

[80] "Gary Zukav Quotes," Goodreads, accessed Jan. 1, 2021, https://www.goodreads.com/author/quotes/26975.Gary_Zukav.

[81] "The Holstee Manifesto," Holstee, accessed December 6, 2021, https://www.holstee.com/pages/manifesto.

[82] "Maya Angelou Quotes," AZ Quotes, accessed Jan. 11, 2021, https://www.azquotes.com/quote/344894.

[83] "The Secret Plot Summary," IMBd, accessed December 5, 2021, https://www.imdb.com/title/tt0846789/plotsummary.

[84] Schucman, 14.

[85] Wayne Dyer, *The Power of Intention: Learning to Co-create Your World Your Way*: Easyread Super Large 20pt Edition (n.c.: CreateSpace, 2009), 355.

[86] Steve Jobs, "'YOUR TIME IS LIMITED, SO DON'T WASTE IT LIVING SOMEONE ELSE'S LIFE': JOBS," First Post, October 06, 2011, https://www.firstpost.com/tech/news-analysis/your-time-is-limited-so-dont-waste-it-living-someone-elses-life-jobs-2-3589139.html.

[87] "Albert Einstein Quotes," Quote Fancy, accessed January 10, 2021, https://quotefancy.com/quote/763343/Albert-Einstein-Everything-is-Energy-and-that-is-all-there-is-to-it-Match-the-frequency.

[88] Wikipedia contributors, "Masaru Emoto," Wikipedia, The Free Encyclopedia, accessed February 10, 2022, https://en.wikipedia.org/w/index.php?title=Masaru_Emoto&oldid=1070271157.

Life Timeline Journal

The *Life Timeline Journal* provides readers with an opportunity to write down their reflections after reading each chapter of Behind the Screen. There are exercises at the end of most chapters with specific questions for the reader to answer. Follow along in the journal as you read and use it to answer the questions of each exercise.

Use the *Life Timeline* as a tool to map out your experiences/memories and realizations when applying the 7-Step System of Transformation:

CHAPTER 1 - REFLECTION:

CHAPTER 2 - REFLECTION:

CHAPTER 3 - REFLECTION:

CHAPTER 4 - EXERCISE 1:
Step 1 - TAG IT!
Refer to Chapter 4, Page 58 in Behind the Screen:

> Do you have a recurring behavior pattern or theme that's been showing up for you? If so, Tag it. Identify on your *Life Timeline* the day you realized this unconscious trait. Typically, this would take place at the moment you become aware, "This is an issue for me." What are some issues that you may need to tag? Relationship issues? Unhealthy behavior patterns? Negative thoughts? Addictions? Forms of escape? What are you trying to escape from?

Brainstorm and list any issues you currently face or negative behavior patterns that are affecting your results in life?

TAG IT! Today's Date: _____

_____
_____
_____
_____
_____
_____
_____
_____
_____
_____

Next, use the following table to list each issue or behavior. In what way is the issue having a negative impact on your life? Rate each issue and how much of an impact it's having on a scale of low impact, medium impact, or high impact.

ISSUE or BEHAVIOR:	IMPACT ON MY LIFE	RATE (LOW, MED, HIGH)
Ex: fear getting hurt/ shut people out	Relationship issues. I've been single for years and long for love.	High

Select the issue or behavior with the highest rating of impact on your life and TAG IT (present day) on your *Life Timeline*:

MY LIFE TIMELINE

Write it down and pin it up on your Life Timeline, the day you "tagged it."

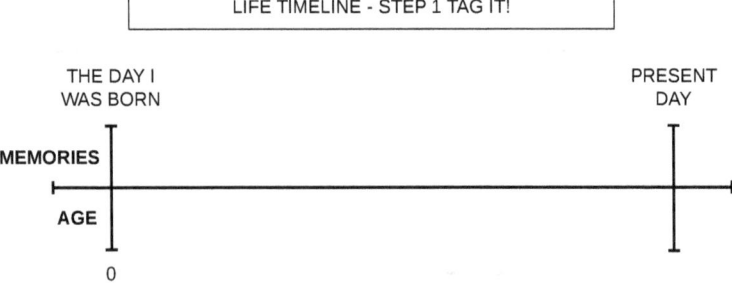

CHAPTER 4 - EXERCISE 2:
Step 2 – REMEMBER IT!
Refer to Chapter 4, Page 58 in Behind the Screen:

After you have tagged your issue, **try to remember the first time you ever experienced this type of behavior or way of thinking.** Go as far back as you can remember.

> This is the neural-circuitry of wiring in your brain that's been a program running on autopilot. Go back and remember the first instance of that tagged issue, behavior, or thought. Maybe it was demonstrated to you by a parent or caretaker? Did you experience trauma or pain that could be related to this perspective? As you learned in Chapter 2, the brain of a child from birth to seven years old is extremely permeable. Challenge yourself to recall back as far as you can to assess **when that way of thinking took root in your subconscious mind.**

Write down the memory of the experience and indicate the age at which this took place on your *Life Timeline*. If you notice that this memory—or another instance that matches the theme—**shows up multiple times, plot each instance on the *Life Timeline* at the age of inception.**

Remember, the story you tell yourself is the movie you produce.
Oftentimes, we repeat stories and unconscious behavior patterns that turn into our reality.

BEHIND THE SCREEN

Explain the first memory and age you experienced it:

_____
_____
_____
_____
_____
_____
_____
_____
_____

List any other experiences and memories of this recurring issue/pattern and the age of inception of each.

_____
_____
_____
_____
_____
_____
_____
_____
_____
_____

LIFE TIMELINE JOURNAL

Use the *Life Timeline* to map out your age and each memory / experience that reflects your issue or pattern. (Example below).

MY LIFE TIMELINE

After applying Step 1 - TAG IT (Fear of Heart Break / Broken Family), list the first memory of this experience and your age. If you experienced this issue multiple times, list each memory and age.

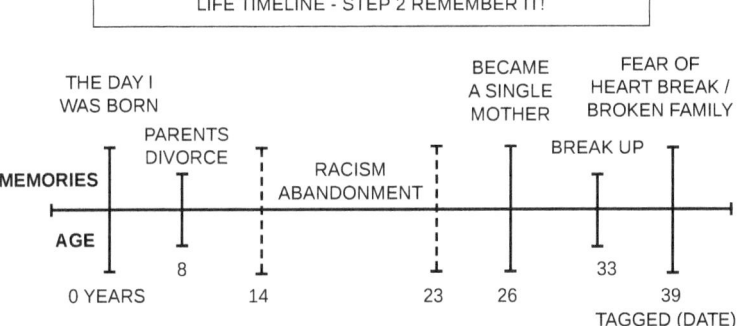

MY LIFE TIMELINE

After applying Step 1 - TAG IT (your issue), list the first memory of this experience and your age.

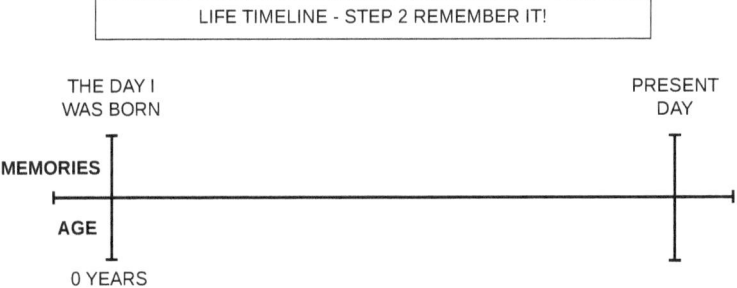

CHAPTER 4 - EXERCISE 3:
Step 3 - FEEL IT!
Refer to Chapter 4, Page 59 in Behind the Screen:

After you have recalled all the memories from your past associated with this topic, **reflect on the way you felt (at that time).** Feel the emotions like you felt them back then.

> This step is not about how you feel today, it's intended to get you to feel the emotions from that past event now. Feel the emotions in order to uproot them from your energy body. **Explore where there may be unprocessed pain, shame, or guilt.** Allow yourself to feel it. Write down the age at which you experienced these emotions. Be descriptive during your journaling process. Take as much time and space as you need to really unpack these memories and emotions.

LIFE TIMELINE JOURNAL

What are your triggers? What or who triggers you to react in a negative way?

_____

_____

_____

_____

_____

_____

_____

_____

_____

Why do you think you react this way?

_____

_____

_____

_____

_____

_____

_____

_____

_____

_____

_____

CHAPTER 5 - EXERCISE 4:
Reflect upon Your Teenage Screen
Refer to Chapter 5, Page 77 in Behind the Screen:

Have you dealt with a similar situation? Heartbreak or Lost Love? If so, how do you feel about it today? What emotions show up when you recall that experience?

_____

_____

_____

_____

_____

_____

_____

When reading this chapter, would you consider yourself as the **empathetic observer, critical judger, or personal player? Why?**

_____

_____

_____

_____

_____

_____

_____

_____

How does your perspective as a teenager differ from your perspective today? Why do you think that is? If you are a teenager, how do you think your perspective may shift later in life?

_____

_____

_____

_____

_____

What type of programming did you download from your teen years?

_____

_____

_____

_____

_____

Apply Steps 1 – 3 if you notice remnants of a program that took root during your adolescence.

_____

_____

_____

_____

_____

CHAPTER 6 - EXERCISE 5:
Projecting Unfulfilled Expectations?
Refer to Chapter 6, Page 81 in Behind the Screen:

Did you experience having any unfulfilled expectations during your adolescence? If so, list them in detail:

_____
_____
_____
_____
_____
_____
_____

Now take a moment to observe where you may feel that same sense of being unfulfilled in your life today. **Could you be projecting unsettled negative emotions or unfulfilled expectations into your current environment or relationships? If so, how, and why? What is the source of this projection?**

_____
_____
_____
_____
_____
_____

Apply Steps 1 – 3 to each scenario that applies. You should also be mapping these memories on your *Life Timeline* in order to uncover patterns that you may not be aware exist.

_____
_____
_____
_____
_____
_____
_____

MY LIFE TIMELINE
Memories / Experiences

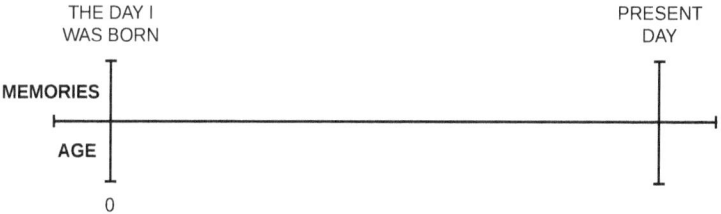

CHAPTER 7 - EXERCISE 6:
The Looking Glass
Refer to Chapter 7, Page 101 in Behind the Screen:

After reading Chapter 7, what ideas or memories came to mind? What insight was reflected back to you?

_____

_____

_____

_____

_____

_____

_____

Have you dealt with any mental health issues? What about someone in your family or a close friend? How has this impacted your life?

_____

_____

_____

_____

_____

_____

_____

What type of belief systems did you inherit?

_____

_____

_____

_____

_____

_____

What experiences did you survive that constructed your character? These are pieces of the puzzle that create your personality and personal reality. Are the pieces serving you now or strangling your ability to find peace and harmony within your *Life Timeline*?

_____

_____

_____

_____

_____

_____

Do you love the person you are on either side of that screen?

_____

_____

_____

_____

_____

If you are a parent, how may you be passing some sort of programming onto your children (or vice versa)?

_____
_____
_____
_____
_____
_____

How are you contributing to the health of our planet?

_____
_____
_____
_____
_____
_____

What could you do differently to make this world a better place?

_____
_____
_____
_____
_____
_____

CHAPTER 8 - EXERCISE 7:
Infinite Possibilities

Refer to Chapter 8, Page 118 in Behind the Screen:

> Remember to think and dream big. Dig deep down into your heart.
> *Connect to the power that is breathing you.*

Reflect on the following questions:
What is possible for you? Your future? Your family?

_____
_____
_____
_____
_____
_____

If you did not allow the expectations and opinions of others to affect your decisions, **what would you do differently?**

_____
_____
_____
_____
_____
_____

BEHIND THE SCREEN

What does peace feel like?

_____
_____
_____
_____
_____

What does happiness look like? What is your soul longing for? What would you love?

_____
_____
_____
_____
_____

What can you do, what will you do, what are you doing or becoming?

"I can... I will... I AM..."

I CAN..._____

I WILL..._____

I AM..._____

CHAPTER 9 - EXERCISE 8:
Step 4 – FLIP IT!
Refer to Chapter 9, Page 124 in Behind the Screen:

> You have already applied Steps 1, 2, 3 to the issues, triggers, or behavior patterns you experience. **Now, apply Step 4 - Flip It**. Look at each experience from a new screen or different perspective.

What comes up for you when you apply Step 4?

_____
_____
_____
_____
_____

What perspective are you able to see differently?

_____
_____
_____
_____
_____
_____

Is there a silver lining or something good that resulted from this experience?

_____
_____
_____
_____
_____
_____
_____
_____
_____

How do you feel when you see the story from the other side?

_____
_____
_____
_____
_____
_____
_____
_____
_____
_____

CHAPTER 10 - REFLECTION:

CHAPTER 11 - EXERCISE 9:
Step 5 - RELEASE IT!
Refer to Chapter 11, Page 156 in Behind the Screen:

Do you have repressed emotions lingering from your past or unprocessed energy that needs to be released? Explain the emotion or unprocessed energy that your subconscious mind/body is holding onto.

_____

_____

_____

_____

_____

_____

_____

_____

_____

_____

_____

_____

_____

_____

_____

_____

_____

_____

Can you identify where this stuck energy may be residing in your body? Do you have physical pain or symptoms as a result?

___

Which form(s) of Energy Release will you commit to trying?

___

When will you commit to doing the Energy Release? Set a date and hold yourself accountable to do the work.

___

Do you feel like you need help or support from a friend or professional? **If so, who will you call on?**

CHAPTER 12 - EXERCISE 10:
What Really Matters?
Refer to Chapter 12, Page 169 in Behind the Screen:

> Are you caught up in a program or way of thinking that is inhibiting your transformation?
> **Ask yourself these questions about what really matters in your life.**

What makes *today* matter? Why?

_____
_____
_____
_____
_____
_____

Where do you spend the majority of your time and attention?

_____
_____
_____
_____
_____
_____
_____

BEHIND THE SCREEN

Why does that matter?

_____
_____
_____
_____
_____
_____

What will matter tomorrow?

_____
_____
_____
_____
_____
_____

What will matter one year from now?

_____
_____
_____
_____
_____
_____

LIFE TIMELINE JOURNAL

Five years from now?

_____
_____
_____
_____
_____
_____
_____
_____

What do you think matters when you take your last breath of air?

- Is it that Michael Kors purse you wanted?
- How well your hair looks or if your nails are done?
- The designer clothes in your closet?
- The type of car you drive?

_____
_____
_____
_____
_____
_____
_____
_____

BEHIND THE SCREEN

What should you do differently?

CHAPTER 13 - EXERCISE 11:
Step 6 - REPROGRAM
Refer to Chapter 13, Page 180 in Behind the Screen:

CREATE A VISION

> Close your eyes. Take a deep breath. Imagine you are walking into the life of your dreams at least **three years from now.** As you enter into a future with limitless potential, remember there is nothing holding you back—no limitations, conditions, or fear. Begin by saying, **"I am so happy and grateful...."** Then envision yourself living your best life. Don't even think about how this will happen. Just see your dream with a childlike imagination. See it, smell it, five-sense it in your mind, body, and soul.

Once you have visualized it, write that vision down in explicit detail.

_____
_____
_____
_____
_____
_____
_____
_____
_____
_____
_____

Next, **speak your vision out loud...** (do so now).

> Your breath will give life to the words. The vibration of your voice fuels the words to flow into the Universe that manifests all existence. The feeling tone of your energy being will tune into the frequency of that channel. **Continue this daily.**

Believe that you can co-create this life because you can, 100 percent! The only thing that will block you from attracting this is your own fear, doubt, or worry. The egoic lens shadows your potential. Delete it from the story.

Believe fully in your dream with your whole mind, body, and soul.
Let the Universe do the work with you.

CHAPTER 13 - EXERCISE 12:
Step 7 – RESONATE
Refer to Chapter 13, Page 185 in Behind the Screen:

BECOME THE NEW YOU!

***Be creative and get excited about this process.
It's fun... and it works.***

As you envision yourself living this new way of life, how do you feel? Describe your state of being and way of feeling...

_____
_____
_____
_____
_____
_____

What makes you feel this way? Be descriptive and detail every feeling or emotion that comes up, so you can assume that feeling tone right away.

_____
_____
_____
_____
_____
_____

What can you do today to feel this way?

_____

_____

_____

_____

_____

_____

What can you do tomorrow and the next day to feel this way?

_____

_____

_____

_____

_____

_____

Do it. Take action. List at least two action steps you will take and by when. Add them to your calendar.

Action 1: _____

Action 1 to be completed by: _____

Action 2: _____

Action 2 to be completed by: _____

CHAPTER 14 - EXERCISE 13:
Take Action
Refer to Chapter 14, Page 197 in Behind the Screen:

Reflect on the following questions after reading Chapter 14:
How do you relate to this story? Have you ever had a wake-up call that interrupted your regularly scheduled program? What was the catalyst that forced you to see clearly?

_____

_____

_____

_____

_____

_____

How can you reflect on that "life lesson" and gain a greater understanding of yourself and what your soul may be seeking? If fear, doubt, or worry were not present in your mind's eye, what would you choose to do differently?

_____

_____

_____

_____

_____

_____

_____

Make a list of at least three action steps that you will take to initiate your transformation.

☐ Action 1:   Due Date:_____

_____

_____

_____

☐ Action 2:   Due Date:_____

_____

_____

_____

☐ Action 3:   Due Date:_____

_____

_____

_____

Be sure to come back here and check the box next to each action step once you complete it.

Celebrate each accomplishment!
Hold yourself accountable to follow through on your goals.
<u>Continue taking action, daily.</u>